IT'S OBVIOUS YOU WON'T SURVIVE
BY YOUR WITS ALONE

Other Dilbert Books from Andrews and McMeel

Andrews and McMeel
A Universal Press Syndicate Company
Kansas City

Introduction

I created the first five Dilbert books strictly to earn money. This sixth book is being done for love. Specifically, my love of money.

I don't mean I "love" money in some greedy, shallow sense of the word. I mean I actually have feelings for money. I once had a fling with an attractive little five dollar bill. It was wonderful, if you don't count the paper cuts . . . and of course there was the big fight after my tasteless joke about Ford's Theater. But mostly it was good.

It ended like most of my relationships — I traded her for a bag of Ruffles and a Diet Coke. The moral of the story is, "Don't fall in love on an empty stomach," especially if your loved one is accepted as legal tender at convenience stores.

Speaking of hunger, at parties I'm often asked if I see myself more as a writer or an artist. To which I reply, "Excuse me while I freshen my Snapple*." Then I scurry away. I escape because the conversation inevitably degenerates into unpleasant comparisons of my artwork and things found in nature, such as carpet stains and motorcycle accidents.

I'm sure my artwork would be better if I spent more time on it, but I'm a busy guy. Take today for instance; I have to write an exciting introduction for this book. Later I'll be sorting all of my currency into "cute" and "ugly" piles. This stuff doesn't happen by itself.

Here's my point: Wouldn't it be nice if all the annoying people on earth became our personal servants? Well, it's possible. As you may already know, when Dogbert conquers the planet and becomes supreme ruler, anybody who is not on the free Dilbert newsletter mailing list will become domestic servants for the enlightened people who are. Save yourself from that fate by joining now.

The Dilbert newsletter is free and it's published approximately "whenever I feel like it," which is about four times a year.

E-mail subscription (preferred): write to scottadams@aol.com

Snail mail: Dilbert Mailing List c/o United Media
                200 Madison Ave.
                New York, NY 10016

Scott Adams

http://www.unitedmedia.com/comics/dilbert/

* It's not what you think. You're disgusting.

DILBERT By Scott Adams

DILBERT, I'D LIKE YOU TO INTRODUCE THE NEW GUY TO EVERYBODY.

GROAN

THIS WAY I NEVER HAVE TO LEARN THEIR NAMES.

THE FIRST STOP ON OUR ODYSSEY IS BUD.

UH... BUD, THIS IS THE NEW GUY, AND VICE-VERSA.

WHAT'S THIS?! ANOTHER PINK-BOTTOMED, IVY LEAGUE, MANAGEMENT "TRAINEE"?!

NEWS

IN MY DAY, YOU HAD TO START AT THE BOTTOM... AND BY GOLLY, YOU STAYED THERE!!

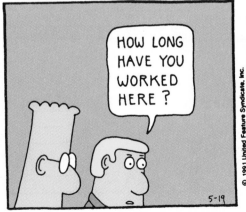

HOW LONG HAVE YOU WORKED HERE?

5-19

© 1991 United Feature Syndicate, Inc.

A WEEK... THIS HAPPENS PRETTY QUICKLY.

9

DILBERT

By Scott Adams

WELCOME TO DOGBERT'S "SCHOOL OF HARD KNOCKS."

THIS IS THE SCHOOL YOU'VE HEARD SO MUCH ABOUT.

CHANCES ARE, ONE OF YOUR PARENTS IS A GRADUATE OF THIS SCHOOL.

© 1991 United Feature Syndicate, Inc.

AT DOGBERT'S SCHOOL OF HARD KNOCKS, YOU WILL GAIN THE WISDOM THAT CAN ONLY BE OBTAINED THROUGH SUFFERING.

THROUGHOUT THE COURSE, I'LL BE WHACKING YOU WITH VARIOUS BLUNT OBJECTS.

IT MAY BE UNPLEASANT AT FIRST, BUT YOU'LL GET USED TO IT.

EVENTUALLY, YOUR BRAIN WILL RATIONALIZE THE WHOLE EXPERIENCE. YOU'LL THINK I'M A DEDICATED TEACHER, AND YOU'LL ACTUALLY BELIEVE YOU LEARNED SOMETHING.

STICK WITH THE BASICS, I SAY.

5-26

THIS SONY SNIFFMAN MAKES A NICE GIFT.

YOU CAN PLAY THE SMELLS OF YOUR FAVORITE STARS!

TRY IT - IT'S DONNY OSMOND'S GYM BAG.

IS IT "NEW DONNY" OR CLASSIC?

THIS IS MY NEW OPTICAL DISK PLAYER FOR THE COMPUTER.

NOW I CAN INSTANTLY ACCESS THE WORKS OF SHAKESPEARE OR STUDY THE HISTORY OF GREECE!

HOW OFTEN DO YOU NEED TO DO THAT?

YOU JUST DON'T UNDERSTAND TECHNOLOGY, DO YOU?

I'M JUST A DOG.

THE DIFFERENCE BETWEEN MEN AND WOMEN

(WELL, ONE OF THEM)

IT'S RAINING!! LET'S GO FROLIC IN THE RAIN!!

FROLIC?

THIS'D BETTER HAVE A HUGE PAYOFF.

14

DOGBERT IS A CONSULTANT

I HAVE AN UNORTHODOX PLAN FOR IMPROVING YOUR IMAGE IN THE COMPANY.

SHOOT.

LUCKY GUESS.

PALM READING $20

YOUR LIFE LINE IS VERY SHORT.

I CAN GET YOU A FEW MORE YEARS BY EXTENDING THE LINE WITH THIS GREASE PENCIL.

SOMEDAY I SHOULD GO BACK AND HAVE HER LENGTHEN MY INTELLIGENCE LINE TOO.

I'D HURRY.

UP I HICC!

UP I HICC!

UP I HICC!
UP I HICC!

ENGLISH TEACHER.

DILBERT

By Scott Adams

WHAT ARE YOU WORKING ON?

I'M WRITING MY OWN ENCYCLOPEDIA TO SELL FOR LARGE PROFITS.

HOW COULD YOU WRITE AN ENTIRE ENCYCLOPEDIA BY YOURSELF?

IT'S ABRIDGED. I HAD TO CUT SOME CORNERS TO GET IT ALL IN FIVE PAGES.

FIVE PAGES?! YOU CONDENSED THE HISTORY AND KNOWLEDGE OF THE WORLD INTO FIVE PAGES?!!

ACTUALLY, IT'S MOSTLY ABOUT ME ... THE OTHER STUFF DIDN'T SEEM IMPORTANT.

6-9

BUT I THREW IN SOME STUFF ABOUT CANADA TO MAKE IT SEEM THOROUGH.

"CANADA HAS TREES."

I'LL HAVE TO TIGHTEN THAT SECTION A BIT.

STARTING TODAY, THE COMPANY WILL BEGIN RANDOM DRUG TESTING.

ALTHOUGH IT WOULD BE ILLEGAL TO SEARCH YOUR CAR OR HOME FOR ILLEGAL DRUGS . . .

WE HAVE FOUND NO ETHICAL PROBLEM WITH SUCKING THE BLOOD OUT OF YOUR BODY.

RESULTS WILL BE POSTED IN THE CAFETERIA.

WHY HAVE YOU REFUSED TO SUBMIT TO OUR EMPLOYEE DRUG TESTING?

IT'S A VIOLATION OF MY PRIVACY AND AN INSULT TO MY INTEGRITY. I DEMAND TO BE JUDGED ONLY ON MY <u>PERFORMANCE</u>.

BUT YOUR PERFORMANCE STINKS.

PERFORMANCE <u>AND</u> ATTENDANCE.

DON'T YOU THINK THE COMPANY'S DRUG TESTING POLICY IS A VIOLATION OF OUR PRIVACY?

I DON'T DO DRUGS.

JOHNSON, YOUR BLOOD TEST RESULTS ARE IN. LOOKS LIKE YOU LIVE ON CHEETOS AND DIET PEPSI . . . YOUR WIFE DOESN'T LOVE YOU . . . AND WHOA . . . WHAT'S THIS?

APPARENTLY, YOU LIKE TO DRESS IN GRASS SKIRTS AND MAKE FUN OF THE LAWNMOWER.

IT'S AN ETHICAL DILEMMA... I SUPPORT MY COMPANY'S GOAL OF DISCOURAGING DRUG USE, BUT THE RANDOM DRUG TESTING POLICY IS A VIOLATION OF MY CONSTITUTIONAL RIGHTS.

I'LL GET FIRED IF I REFUSE THE TEST. WHAT IS THE ETHICAL THING TO DO?

HACK INTO THEIR COMPUTER AND CHANGE YOUR BOSS'S TEST RESULTS.

SOMETIMES THE STRAIGHTEST PATH IS THROUGH THE MUD.

GOOD, RATIONALIZE IT WITH AN OBTUSE METAPHOR.

I'M DISCONTINUING THE EMPLOYEE DRUG TESTING PROGRAM...

BECAUSE MY OWN TESTS KEEP TURNING OUT POSITIVE ... WHICH MAKES ME SUSPECT THAT SOME WISE-GUY HAS TAMPERED WITH THE MEDICAL COMPUTER.

DENIAL AND PARANOIA... CLASSIC SYMPTOMS.

IS HE "HIGH" RIGHT NOW?

I'VE BEEN THINKING ABOUT MY GOAL OF BECOMING THE SUPREME RULER OF EARTH...

I KNOW EXACTLY HOW YOU FEEL. I ONCE HAD A GOAL OF GROWING A MUSTACHE ... BUT IT WAS BEYOND MY GRASP.

I MEAN, FIGURATIVELY BEYOND MY GRASP. I COULD STILL REACH MY UPPER LIP, YOU UNDERSTAND ... BUT THERE WAS NO REASON TO TRY.

RIGHT, BUT BACK TO ME...

I THOUGHT IT WAS BAD WHEN THEY MADE US WORK IN THOSE LITTLE CUBICLES...

THEN THEY PUT TWO PEOPLE IN EACH CUBICLE... BUT WE GOT USED TO IT.

I GUESS WE'LL GET USED TO VELCRO STRIPS, TOO.

I'VE SOLVED AN ANCIENT PUZZLE..

I FIGURED OUT HOW MANY ANGELS CAN DANCE ON THE HEAD OF A PIN!

I DON'T CARE WHAT HE THINKS ...THE ANSWER IS SIX.

I'M STARTING MY OWN TABLOID NEWSPAPER, THE "DOGBERT STAR."

ALL OF THE STORIES WILL BE SENSATIONAL LIES ABOUT ME... THAT WAY I'LL SAVE MONEY ON LAWSUITS.

"AN ANGRY DOGBERT DENIED THAT HIS EGO WAS SO BIG HE STARTED A TABLOID DEVOTED ENTIRELY TO HIMSELF."

DOGBERT STARTS A TABLOID NEWSPAPER DEVOTED TO LIES ABOUT HIMSELF

WHERE DO YOU GET YOUR IDEAS?

"DOGBERT'S IMPATIENCE WITH FOOLS WAS LEGENDARY. HE ONCE CHOKED A MAN BY HIS NECKTIE FOR ASKING STUPID QUESTIONS."

"IT HAPPENED ONE DAY WHEN THE FOOL WAS READING OVER DOGBERT'S SHOULDER AND GOT TOO CLOSE."

IT'S GOING TO BE ANOTHER YEAR OF FLOGGING DEAD HORSES.

BUT SOMEHOW WE'LL MUDDLE THROUGH OUR INTERNAL BUREAUCRACY, GOUGE OUR CUSTOMERS, AND KEEP GETTING OUR TINY PAYCHECKS.

SIR, WILSON TURNED INTO A CLUMP OF UNINSPIRED SOD.

IT'S JUST AS WELL; HE HAD A BAD ATTITUDE.

YOU KNOW THAT GOOD FEELING YOU GET WHEN YOU FIRST PUT A Q-TIP IN YOUR EAR?

YEAH.

CAN I FREELY ENJOY IT, OR IS IT A SIN?

I THINK IT'S OKAY.

GOOD, BECAUSE I USED A WHOLE BOX YESTERDAY.

DILBERT

By Scott Adams

ADD ONE JAR OF SPAGHETTI SAUCE...

HMPH
GRRR
UNH

RRRRR

LET ME TRY TO HUMILIATE YOU BY OPENING IT EASILY.

THIS DEFINITELY WOULD HAVE WORKED IN "FAMILY CIRCUS."

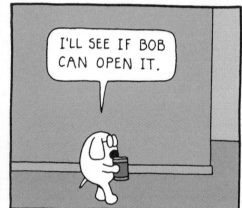

I'LL SEE IF BOB CAN OPEN IT.

NO PROBLEM FOR A MIGHTY DINOSAUR.

6-23

SMASH!

WILL YOU STOP HUMMING "MY WAY."

S. Adams

YOU'VE BEEN RANDOMLY SELECTED TO HAVE LUNCH WITH A SENIOR EXECUTIVE OF THE COMPANY.

THIS IS HOW THE EXECUTIVES SHOW THAT THEY ARE REGULAR PEOPLE, JUST LIKE YOU AND ME.

AT LUNCH

I COULD SQUASH YOU LIKE A BUG! HA HA HA HA HA HA!

DILBERT IS CHOSEN TO HAVE LUNCH WITH AN EXECUTIVE.

I WANT YOU TO KNOW THAT I'M JUST A NORMAL GUY...

OH, SURE, I MAKE A LITTLE MORE MONEY, AND I HAVE A NICE OFFICE...

AND OF COURSE, I'M MUCH, MUCH SMARTER.

LUNCH WITH A TOP EXECUTIVE

I HAVE THESE LUNCHES TO FIND OUT WHAT THE WORKERS ARE THINKING. YOU MAY SPEAK FREELY.

OKAY... IT SEEMS LIKE THE COMPANY IS LACKING LEADERSHIP AND DIRECTION. THE EXECUTIVES SQUELCH ALL INITIATIVE BY PUNISHING THOSE WHO TAKE RISKS AND VOICE OPINIONS.

YOU LEAVE ME LITTLE CHOICE BUT TO FLING THIS AU GRATIN POTATO AT YOUR FOREHEAD.

DILBERT

By Scott Adams

I'VE HIRED A CONSULTANT TO CLARIFY OUR COMPANY POLICY ON DISCRIMINATION.

IT IS AGAINST POLICY TO DISCRIMINATE BASED ON RACE, SEX, AGE, HANDICAP OR RELIGION

CONSULTANT

DOES THAT INCLUDE UNPOPULAR, LITTLE RELIGIONS?

NO, THOSE ARE CONSIDERED CULTS; YOU MAY DISCRIMINATE FREELY AGAINST THEM.

WHAT ABOUT SHORT, BALD, FAT, UGLY MEN? ARE THEY CONSIDERED "HANDICAPPED"?

TECHNICALLY, NO. YOU CAN STILL TEASE THEM AND DENY THEM PROMOTIONS AS USUAL.

LIKEWISE, YOU MAY DISCRIMINATE AGAINST NERDS, SMOKERS, AND SINGLE PEOPLE.

AND WE'VE DROPPED "STUPID PEOPLE" FROM THE WATCH LIST, AS THEIR LOBBYING EFFORTS PROVED INEFFECTIVE...

6-30

DILBERT CELEBRATES HIS VICTORY IN COURT.

YES!!

PUT ME DOWN.

HA HA! I'M FREE! NO MORE SIX-BY-SIX PRISON CELL!

AAH... IT FEELS SO GOOD TO HAVE MY FREEDOM AND INDIVIDUALITY BACK.

I HAVEN'T BEEN ABLE TO GET A JOB IN TWO YEARS.

IT'S BECAUSE EVERYBODY KNOWS MY BROTHER IS IN JAIL. PEOPLE THINK I MUST BE DISHONEST TOO.

YOU SHOULD NOT JUDGE A COOK BY ITS BROTHER.

HE PROBABLY SAYS THE SAME ABOUT YOU.

THE MORE I WATCH TELEVISION, THE MORE I WONDER WHY I'M NOT ALREADY SUPREME RULER OF EARTH.

THOSE PEOPLE ARE IDIOTS. THEY SHOULD ALL DRIVE OVER HERE AND PROCLAIM ME THEIR KING.

THE SECRET TO HAPPINESS IS HIGH EXPECTATIONS AND YOUR OWN BAG OF CHIPS.

WHO WOULD WIN IF A GIANT MOTH FOUGHT A GIANT BUT MODEST BEE IN AN ALL-WOOL JUMPSUIT?

WAIT... WHO'S WEARING THE JUMPSUIT -- THE GIANT MOTH OR THE GIANT BEE?

THE BEE.

IS THIS JUST HYPOTHETICAL?

I CAN'T STOP PUTTING WRITING TOOLS IN MY SHIRT POCKET...

IT STARTED HARMLESSLY... FIRST A PEN, THEN TWO. NOW I'M AFRAID TO GO ANYWHERE WITHOUT A PEN AND PENCIL OF EVERY COLOR.

DO YOU HAVE THE SECONDARY COLORS?

THERE ARE SECONDARY COLORS?!

I BOUGHT SOME MUD FLAPS WITH THE SILHOUETTE OF A NAKED WOMAN.

WITH THESE ON MY CAR, WOMEN WILL THINK I'M A SEXIST NEANDER-THAL, AND MEN WILL BE EMBARRASSED TO SHARE MY GENDER.

BUT NOW I'M HAVING SECOND THOUGHTS.

THAT IMPLIES YOU HAD FIRST THOUGHTS.

DILBERT

By Scott Adams

WHY DO DOGS TWITCH THEIR FEET WHEN THEY SLEEP?

ZZZZ

IT'S SO CUTE. THEY MUST BE DREAMING ABOUT CHASING CARS.

HA HA! I AM SAINT DOGBERT! LINE UP TO KISS MY FEET, YOU KNAVES!

WHAT'S ON MY SCHEDULE TODAY, LACKEY?

YOU'LL BE PUSHING WHINEY, UGLY PEOPLE INTO MUD AT NINE.

7-14

THEN, YOU'LL TEASE CATS ABOUT THEIR GROOMING METHODS UNTIL TEN.

GOOD, GOOD.

THEN YOU'LL RAISE TAXES, GO TO LUNCH, AND TAKE THE REST OF THE DAY OFF.

REALITY: WHAT A GYP.

S.Adams

Ratbert's Journal
Day one: I have disguised myself as a chihuahua so I can experience their lifestyle and make a movie.

I have already seen the senseless prejudice and brutality against an innocent chihuahua.

This morning I slapped myself with a rolled up newspaper for no apparent reason. It was strangely satisfying.

HEY, AREN'T YOU ONE OF THOSE CHIHUAHUA DOGS?

THE DISGUISE IS WORKING.

UNLESS... MAYBE YOU'RE JUST A RAT IN A TURTLENECK SWEATER, PRETENDING TO BE A CHIHUAHUA.

THINK FAST.

I DON'T HAVE THE ATTENTION SPAN TO THINK ABOUT IT.

WHAT DID HE MEAN BY "JUST A RAT"?

RATBERT! WHAT HAPPENED TO YOU?

MY CHIHUAHUA DISGUISE WORKED. I'VE BEEN TAUNTED AND CHASED ALL DAY BY BIGOTS WHO HATE CHIHUAHUAS FOR NO REASON.

THERE'S AN IMPORTANT LESSON IN THIS.

WHAT? CHIHUAHUAS ARE EVIL?

DILBERT

By Scott Adams

WOOOOOOOOOO

POLICE?

YOU MADE AN ILLEGAL U-TURN.

YOU'RE GIVING ME A TICKET FOR THAT?! A MEASLY U-TURN?!

I CAN'T BELIEVE IT! THE WORLD IS FULL OF MURDERERS AND THUGS, BUT YOU STOP ME?

I'M WASTING MY TAXES ON YOUR SALARY!

AND FRANKLY, THOSE MUSTACHES YOU GUYS ALL GROW DON'T MAKE YOU LOOK ANY SMARTER.

© 1991 United Feature Syndicate, Inc.

7-21

PLEASE STEP OUT OF YOUR CAR FOR THE SOBRIETY TEST.

...SO, IT TURNS OUT THAT THE SOBRIETY TEST INVOLVES FLINGING YOURSELF DOWN A MUDDY EMBANKMENT.

HOW DID YOU DO IN THE STAND-UP COMEDY COMPETITION?

I WAS HALFWAY THROUGH MY FIRST JOKE -- ABOUT OLD PEOPLE, WHEN AN ELDERLY WOMAN DRAGGED ME OFF STAGE AND SLAPPED THE BEJEEZUS OUT OF ME.

...IT WAS GOOD ENOUGH FOR THIRD PLACE.

WILL YOU SIGN MY PETITION?

WHAT'S IT FOR, BOB?

I DIDN'T HAVE ANY COMPLAINTS, SO IT JUST SAYS "D-UHH."

DEMOCRACY IS A WONDERFUL THING.

FORGOT MY KEYS.

I'LL HAVE TO SLAP MY FOREHEAD AND MUTTER WHEN I TURN AROUND, OTHERWISE I'LL LOOK SILLY.

TOO HARD.

SMACK

I'VE DECIDED TO BECOME A POP PSYCHOLOGIST AND LECTURER.

MY THEORY IS THAT YOU CAN BLAME ALL OF YOUR PROBLEMS ON INVISIBLE PEOPLE.

7-29

THAT DOESN'T SOUND HEALTHY.

DON'T BLAME ME. TALK TO JUAN AND CINDY.

I'VE DECIDED TO BECOME A POP PSYCHOLOGIST. I NEED YOUR HELP TO MAKE MY LECTURE VIDEO.

YOU CAME TO THE RIGHT PLACE, BABE. FIRST, YOU NEED A NEW LOOK.

NICE TRY, BUT FRANKLY, THIS LOOK DIDN'T WORK TOO WELL FOR MADONNA EITHER.

7-30

WELCOME TO THE DOGBERT LECTURE SERIES ON GUILT.

7-31

IN THE NEXT HOUR, YOU WILL LEARN HOW TO COPE WITH GUILT THE DOGBERT WAY.

AND IF YOU DON'T, WELL, IT TURNS OUT I GET PAID ANYWAY.

YOU CAN FREE YOUR-SELF FROM GUILT WITH THE COPYRIGHTED DOGBERT METHOD.

MY METHOD IS SO SIMPLE THAT EVEN STUPID PEOPLE CAN DO IT.

DO WE HAVE ANY STUPID PEOPLE HERE TODAY?

THE DOGBERT METHOD OF ELIMINATING GUILT IS QUITE SIMPLE.

ALL OF YOUR PROBLEMS ARE CAUSED BY INVISIBLE PEOPLE NAMED JUAN AND CINDY.

ALL YOU HAVE TO DO IS FIND THEM AND KILL THEM.

I FEEL LIKE I'M BEING JUDGED BY EVERYBODY I SEE.

WHY CAN'T PEOPLE ACCEPT OTHER PEOPLE AS THEY ARE, WITHOUT JUDGING THEM?

IT WAS A GOOD SPEECH, BUT IT LACKED EMOTION.

7.5

DILBERT

By Scott Adams

UH-OH... THAT GUY IS COMING TO TALK TO US.

I HATE THIS LONG WALK ACROSS THE ROOM.

YOU'RE THE UGLY ONE, EDNA. YOU'LL HAVE TO PROTECT ME.

THEY SPOTTED ME. THEY'RE PLANNING A DEFENSE.

I'LL PUSH YOU BETWEEN US. YOU START BABBLING ABOUT YOUR CAT OR SOMETHING.

I CAN'T DO IT. I'LL VEER OFF AT THE LAST MINUTE...

NOW, EDNA!

IT'S HARD TO BE THE PRETTY ONE.

I HAVE A CAT NAMED BOOTS.

I GOT A JOB AS A USED CAR SALES-MAN.

DOES IT PAY WELL?

I'M NOT IN IT FOR THE MONEY. I JUST ENJOY LYING TO STRANGERS.

8-12

THIS ONE WAS OWNED BY CARLOS THE DIAMOND SMUGGLER. IT CORNERS WELL, BUT THE GAS MILEAGE IS BAD -- ALMOST AS IF IT HAS WEIGHTS HIDDEN IN THE DOOR PANELS.

© 1991 United Feature Syndicate, Inc.

DOGBERT THE CAR SALESMAN

I CAN LET YOU HAVE THIS ONE FOR FIVE THOUSAND.

THREE THOUSAND.

NO, BUT I COULD SELL THAT CAR FOR FOUR THOUSAND.

THIRTY-FIVE HUNDRED.

SOLD.

8-13

I GUESS YOU DON'T GET A LOT OF NEGOTIATORS LIKE ME.

IT'S THE FIRST TIME ANYBODY BOUGHT THE CAR THEY CAME HERE IN.

© 1991 United Feature Syndicate, Inc.

DOGBERT THE USED CAR SALESMAN

WILL THIS BE YOUR FIRST CAR, TIMMY?

YES, SIR... I SAVED MY MONEY FROM MOWING LAWNS.

LET'S SEE HOW MUCH YOU HAVE AND THEN I'LL PICK A CAR FOR YOU.

DO YOU LIKE MOWING LAWNS, TIMMY?

IT'S OKAY.

GOOD, BECAUSE I DON'T RECOM-MEND MED SCHOOL FOR YOU.

8-14

© 1991 United Feature Syndicate, Inc.

DOGBERT THE USED CAR SALESMAN

I ASKED THE BOSS TO SELL IT AT YOUR PRICE.

HE TOLD ME TO DRIVE OVER YOUR FOOT AND STEAL YOUR PURSE.

BUT MAYBE I CAN CONVINCE HIM TO TAKE YOUR FIRST-BORN SON INSTEAD.

HE IS MY FIRST-BORN SON!!

DOGBERT THE USED CAR SALESMAN.

HOW ABOUT THIS ONE?

I DON'T WANT TO SPEND MUCH. I'M ONLY GOING TO TAKE IT APART AND LEAVE IT ON THE LAWN.

I GOTTA BE ME.

I QUIT MY JOB AS A USED CAR SALESMAN.

BECAUSE YOU COULDN'T KEEP LYING?

NO, THE LYING WAS GOOD. I LIKED THAT PART.

WAS IT BECAUSE CRIME DOESN'T PAY?

I MADE $400,000 THIS WEEK. I'M RETIRED NOW.

I DON'T THINK THIS WILL EVER BE A "READER'S DIGEST" VERY SPECIAL STORY.

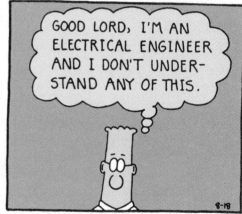

I LOST MY FORTUNE IN A HIGH-RISK INVESTMENT.

JUNK BONDS?

CHECKING ACCOUNT AT "ETHEL'S SAVINGS AND LOAN"!

I'M FROM THE GOVERNMENT. WE'RE REPAYING INSURED DEPOSITORS WHO LOST MONEY IN "ETHEL'S S+L."

WE'RE A LITTLE SHORT ON CASH OURSELVES, SO WE'RE DIVVYING UP THE ITEMS ETHEL BOUGHT.

I GOT A SENATOR.

NOW THAT YOU OWN A SENATOR, WHAT ARE YOU GOING TO DO WITH HIM?

HE'LL APPRECIATE IN VALUE WHEN A CLOSE VOTE COMES UP IN THE SENATE. THEN I'LL SELL HIM TO A POLITICAL ACTION COMMITTEE.

THIS IS STARTING TO AFFECT MY BLIND FAITH IN THE SYSTEM.

HE'S HUNGRY. DO WE HAVE ANY WHISKEY?

DILBERT

By Scott Adams

VIDEO SALES

I'LL TAKE THIS ONE.

WHY WOULD ANY-BODY BUY A MYSTERY MOVIE ?!

WHAT DO YOU DO, WATCH IT A HUNDRED TIMES AND ACT SURPRISED AT THE ENDING ?

GET A LIFE.

I'LL TAKE THIS ONE.

8-25

TOOTSIE ?! YOU WANT TO OWN A MOVIE ABOUT A MAN WHO WEARS DRESSES ?!

© 1991 United Feature Syndicate, Inc.

WHAT ?! I THOUGHT IT WAS A DOCUMENTARY ABOUT TOOTSIE ROLLS. YOU SHOULD LABEL THOSE THINGS MORE CLEARLY !

S.Adams

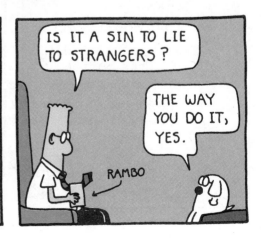

IS IT A SIN TO LIE TO STRANGERS ?

THE WAY YOU DO IT, YES.

RAMBO

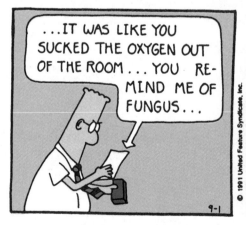

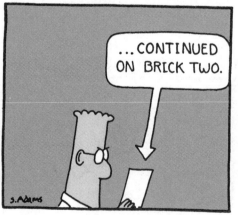

DILBERT, THIS IS YOUR NEW CO-WORKER, FLOYD REMORA.

FLOYD HAS WORKED HERE FOR TWENTY YEARS WITHOUT DEVELOPING ANY SKILLS. HE SURVIVES BY ATTACHING HIMSELF TO THE BACKS OF OTHER EMPLOYEES.

9-2

GO AHEAD... ASK ME HOW MY DAY WENT.

I SEE IT'S YOUR TURN TO WORK WITH FLOYD.

YEAH.

HE LIVED ON MY BACK FOR A YEAR, SHARING MY SUCCESSES WITHOUT CONTRIBUTING.

9-3

I HAD HIM LANCED.

DOES IT LEAVE A BIG HICKEY?

I DON'T MEAN TO SOUND CRITICAL ON A FIRST DATE, BUT THERE'S A LITTLE MAN ATTACHED TO YOUR BACK.

THAT'S FLOYD. HE'S A CO-WORKER WHO SURVIVES BY SHARING THE SUCCESS OF OTHERS.

9-4

WHAT IF YOU'RE NOT SUCCESSFUL?

HE'LL DIE. BUT HEY, NO PRESSURE.

DILBERT

By Scott Adams

"IS THIS THE MEETING?"

"MUMBLE MUMBLE"

"GOOD"

"EVERYBODY TAKE A COPY OF THE AGENDA."

"I'M IN THE WRONG MEETING... NOW IT'S TOO AWKWARD TO LEAVE."

"I'LL CASUALLY STRETCH MY ARMS, FLICK THE LIGHTS OFF AND ESCAPE UNDER COVER OF DARK."

"OUCH! OUCH! OUCH!"

"OH, SORRY, WRONG AGENDA."

"I'M STARTING TO THINK THAT THE PROBLEM WITH OUR ECONOMY IS DEEPER THAN HIGH INTEREST RATES."

HOW DO WE KNOW THAT THE NEWS ISN'T FAKED IN HOLLYWOOD?

WHY IS THERE EXACTLY THIRTY MINUTES OF WORLD NEWS EVERY NIGHT? AND WHY DON'T MAJOR STORIES EVER HAPPEN ON WEEKENDS?

AND I'M SURE I SEE A STRING ATTACHED TO THE SPACE SHUTTLE.

WORSE YET, IT'S A RERUN.

SERIOUSLY, HOW DO WE KNOW THE NEWS ISN'T ALL FAKED??

GEEZ, DOGBERT, GET OVER IT. WHY DON'T YOU JUST CALL GEORGE LUCAS AND ASK HIM IF HE'S DOING THE WHOLE THING WITH SPECIAL EFFECTS?

LUCAS RANCH

WE BUILT A NEW DAN RATHER, BUT IT STILL DOESN'T LOOK LIFE-LIKE.

THERE'S A DOG HERE TO SEE YOU, SIR. HE MAY BE ON TO OUR OPERATION.

George Lucas

YES?

I CAME TO FIND OUT IF THE NEWS ON TELEVISION IS ALL FAKED BY YOUR SPECIAL EFFECTS COMPANY.

ACTUALLY, WE DON'T DO ALL OF THE NEWS HERE. WE HAD TO SUB-CONTRACT THE DAN QUAYLE STUFF TO THE MUPPETS.

I KNEW THAT.

DILBERT

By Scott Adams

DOGBERT, THIS IS MY NEW CO-WORKER, JOHN SMITH.

YO

YO

I INVITED HIM OVER TO WATCH TELEVISION. HE DOESN'T HAVE CABLE YET.

NEXT ON "AMERICA'S MOST WANTED."

THIS MAN GAVE "WEDGIES" TO AN ENTIRE TOWN, ONE PERSON AT A TIME.

Alias: JOHN SMITH

THE VICTIMS WERE WEDGIED IN THEIR OWN HOMES, USUALLY WHILE WATCHING THIS SHOW.

9-15

CAN YOU LEAN OVER AND ADJUST THAT PICTURE?

SURE.

THEY DON'T EVEN EXPLAIN WHAT A WEDGIE IS.

© 1991 United Feature Syndicate, Inc.

THIS IS EXACTLY WHY I DON'T INVITE PEOPLE OVER MORE OFTEN.

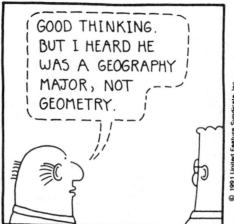

DILBERT

By Scott Adams

MY HOVER-SAUCER INVENTION IS COMPLETE!

IT HAS ENOUGH ADVANCED WEAPONRY TO DESTROY A SMALL COUNTRY.

I HOPE IT DOESN'T FALL INTO THE WRONG HANDS.

PAWS

KNOCK KNOCK

DOGBERT, I AM "FATE." YOU MUST STEAL DILBERT'S HOVER-SAUCER AND CONQUER THE TINY NATION OF ELBONIA.

SINCE WHEN DOES FATE KNOCK?

I WAS BOUGHT OUT IN AN UNFRIENDLY MERGER BY "OPPORTUNITY." I SHOULD HAVE SEEN IT COMING.

IT IS MY DESTINY TO CONQUER ELBONIA USING DILBERT'S HOVER-SAUCER INVENTION.

I FEEL INTOXICATED WITH POWER AND BLINDED BY MY OWN AMBITION.

MAYBE I SHOULDN'T DRIVE WHILE UNDER THE INFLUENCE OF METAPHORS.

IN WORLD NEWS, THE TINY COUNTRY OF ELBONIA HAS BECOME A DESPOTIC MONARCHY.

THE NEW RULER IS KING DOGBERT, WHO CLAIMS TO BE A DESCENDANT OF THE ELBONIAN DEITY "DOUG."

I HOPE THIS DOESN'T GO TO MY HEAD.

WHACK WHACK WHACK

10-7

GIVE ME ONE TICKET FOR THE SLINGSHOT FLIGHT TO ELBONIA'S CAPITAL.

AIR ELBONI

DO YOU WANT FIRST CLASS OR COACH?

WHAT'S THE DIFFERENCE?

10-8

WITH FIRST CLASS WE DON'T INTENTIONALLY FLING YOU TOWARD SOMETHING HARD.

I WISH THERE WERE AN EASIER WAY TO FLY IN ELBONIA.

I'VE GOT TO FIND DOGBERT AND CONVINCE HIM TO STOP BEING THE DESPOTIC RULER OF ELBONIA.

BUT, SIRE, THIS IS THE AIRPORT, NOT THE SKEET-SHOOTING RANGE.

PULL!

10-9

DILBERT LANDS IN ELBONIA WITHOUT HIS SUITCASE.

SPLOIT

10-10

YOU BAGGED A NICE PIECE OF LUGGAGE, M'LORD.

I LIKE TO THINK THIS HELPS MAINTAIN THE DELICATE BALANCE OF NATURE.

YES, SIRE.

I'VE GOT TO CONVINCE HIM TO RESIGN.

KING DOGBERT

I FOUND HIM LURKING, SIRE. THE USUAL PUNISHMENT?

DILBERT!

DOGBERT!

10-11

WHAT IS THE USUAL PUNISHMENT?

A BLIND DATE WITH "EDNA THE LONELIEST HUN."

YOU'VE GOT TO STEP DOWN AS KING OF ELBONIA. THESE PEOPLE ARE CAPABLE OF MAKING THEIR OWN DECISIONS.

THE PAPER-ROCK-SCISSORS OLYMPICS ARE CANCELED. WE COULDN'T AGREE ON THE RULES.

10-12

AND OF COURSE, WE ALL WEAR MITTENS...

WHAT WAS YOUR POINT?

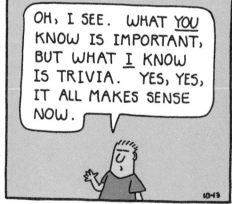

DILBERT By Scott Adams

LOOK! A BEAUTIFUL REGENCY BUTTERFLY!

BEAUTIFUL?? IT'S A FLYING UG.

IT MAY NOT SEEM LIKE MUCH NOW...

BUT AFTER WE KILL IT, DIP IT IN CHEMICALS, AND FLATTEN IT BETWEEN GLASS, IT BECOMES A BEAUTIFUL WORK OF ART!

DO WE THROW AWAY THE BUG GUTS AND JUST KEEP THE WINGS?

NO. THE GUTS KEEP THE WINGS EVENLY SPACED.

EEOW!!! ANTS IN MY PANTS!!

MOTHER NATURE!

HE WAS STANDING RIGHT ON AN ANTHILL. I COULDN'T RESIST.

© 1991 United Feature Syndicate, Inc.

75

UH... WALLY, YOU'RE WEARING ONLY UNDERWEAR AT WORK.

I'M TRYING TO GET FIRED.

THE COMPANY LAYOFF PLAN IS VERY GENEROUS. I'LL GET A BIG PILE OF MONEY IF THEY ASK ME TO LEAVE.

THIS HAS GIVEN ME A DEGREE OF FREEDOM IN DEALING WITH LOCAL MANAGEMENT.

ANY LUCK TRYING TO GET FIRED?

NO... BUT I'LL GET THAT SEVERANCE PACKAGE YET.

THIS MORNING I KRAZY-GLUED FARM ANIMALS TO THE BOSS, BUT HE STILL WON'T DEAL WITH ALL THE BUREAUCRACY TO FIRE ME.

THE STAFF MEETING MAY RUN A LITTLE LONG TODAY.

I HAVEN'T LOOKED AT MY HIGH SCHOOL YEARBOOK IN AGES.

THERE'S MIKE — VOTED MOST LIKELY TO SUCCEED... AND LUCY — VOTED MOST BEAUTIFUL...

WHERE ARE YOU?

DILBERT—"MOST LIKELY TO FIND A POTATO THAT RESEMBLES HIMSELF."

WHO HASN'T?

THIS HIGH SCHOOL YEARBOOK REALLY BRINGS BACK THE MEMORIES.

THERE'S DOPEY BOBBY NOOBER. EVERY DAY WE'D TIE HIM TO THE FLAGPOLE AND STUFF LIVE FROGS IN HIS PANTS.

WHERE IS HE NOW?

HE'S STILL THE PRINCIPAL... NOT THE HAPPIEST GUY I'VE EVER KNOWN.

10-24

WE'VE GOT TO FOCUS MORE ON THE NEEDS OF OUR CUSTOMERS.

I'VE HIRED FAMOUS BUSINESS CONSULTANT TOM PETERS TO FOLLOW YOU AROUND AND MAKE PASSIONATE CRITICISM.

IS THIS QUALITY? ARE YOU TRULY FOCUSED ON THE CUSTOMER?

GREAT... HE'S A SPITTER.

10-25

I HAVE NO LUCK.

YOU KNOW WHAT THEY SAY, "IF LIFE GIVES YOU LEMONS, MAKE LEMONADE."

10-26

I'M ALLERGIC TO CITRUS.

YOU KNOW WHAT THEY SAY, "IF LIFE GIVES YOU LEMONS, SWELL UP AND DIE."

DILBERT

By Scott Adams

DOGBERT'S WORLD OF THE UNEXPLAINED

I'M AT THE FARM OF KAY AND CLEM BOVINSKI...

...THE LOCATION OF UNEXPLAINED PHENOMENA.

(DEEP VOICE) THE DISTURBANCES HAVE LASTED 40 YEARS

OBJECTS MOVE ALL BY THEMSELVES. SOMETIMES THEY HIT CLEM.

I RECKON IT'S POLTERGEIST. NO OTHER EXPLANATION MAKES SENSE.

BONK!

CUT.

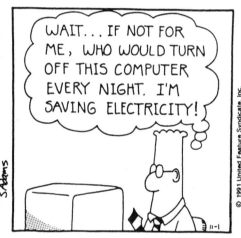

DILBERT

By Scott Adams

SOMEBODY LEFT A PENCIL IN THE ELECTRIC SHARPENER.

THAT'S "EXCALIBERT."

LEGEND HAS IT THAT WHOEVER CAN REMOVE EXCALIBERT FROM THE SHARPENER WILL BECOME CEO.

LIKE THIS?

CONTINUED...

YOU DID IT! YOU REMOVED THE PENCIL "EXCALIBERT" FROM THE SHARPENER.

AS CORPORATE LEGEND REQUIRED, DILBERT BECAME CEO.

HE IMMEDIATELY SET ABOUT THE TASK OF MAKING IMPORTANT DECISIONS.

HERE'S THE LIST OF PEOPLE WHO DIDN'T GROVEL SUFFICIENTLY.

NOW THAT I'M C E O WHAT AM I SUPPOSED TO ACTUALLY DO?

YOU'RE SUPPOSED TO MAKE SUPERFICIAL STATEMENTS ABOUT HOW GOOD THE COMPANY IS, THEN HOPE SOMETHING LUCKY HAPPENS AND PROFITS GO UP.

IT'S CALLED LEADERSHIP, SIR.

MAKE IT SO.

NOW THAT I'M C E O, EVERYBODY TREATS ME DIFFERENTLY.

THEY INTERPRET AND ACT UPON MY SLIGHTEST GESTURE. THIS GESTURE MEANS "ALL IS WELL."

CRASH AAAAGH!

WE TOSSED MAHONEY OUT THE WINDOW LIKE YOU GESTURED, SIR.

OOPS.

11-7

THE JAPANESE HAVE MADE AN OFFER TO BUY THE COMPANY.

AS C E O YOU WOULD MAKE $68 MILLION... BUT THE EMPLOYEES WOULD ALL BE LAID OFF.

IF I ACCEPT, WHAT WILL I SAY TO THE EMPLOYEES?

HOW ABOUT "NEENER NEENER"?

I'VE DECIDED TO REJECT YOUR GENEROUS OFFER TO BUY THE COMPANY.

AND IF YOU TRY TO MAKE THIS A HOSTILE TAKEOVER YOU WILL FIND ME TO BE A FORMIDABLE ADVERSARY.

11-9

...THEN THEIR LAWYERS CHEWED MY CLOTHES OFF.

DILBERT

By Scott Adams

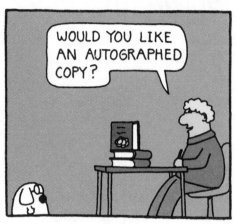

BOOK SIGNING TODAY

WOULD YOU LIKE AN AUTOGRAPHED COPY?

WHO ARE YOU?

I'M BOBBY MCNEWTON, CHILD-STAR FROM THE SIXTIES. I ONCE HAD A SPEAKING PART ON "LEAVE IT TO BEAVER."

I'M LEVERAGING MY FAME TO PROMOTE MY RECIPE BOOK.

Bobby McNewton's Cooking With Walnuts

"WALNUTS AND MILK: CRUSH WALNUTS ON TABLE. POUR MILK ON WALNUTS. SERVE COLD."

"WALNUTS AND PORK: KILL A PIG. COOK DEAD PIG. SPRINKLE WALNUTS ON PIG'S CORPSE."

11-10

I USED A GHOST WRITER.

WAS HE A GHOST BEFORE HE ATE YOUR FOOD?

I STEPPED DOWN AS C E O AND TOOK MY OLD JOB BACK — IT'S LESS STRESSFUL.

SOMETIMES YOU HAVE TO STOP AND SMELL THE ROSES.

EXACTLY.

TOO BAD WE CAN'T AFFORD ANY ROSES NOW.

AS MY DOG, I THINK YOU SHOULD BE DOING MORE TO HELP ME MEET ATTRACTIVE SINGLE WOMEN DURING OUR WALKS.

TRY TO BE CUTER, AND LOOK MORE PET-ABLE.

AND IT'S NOT FUNNY WHEN YOU DO YOUR IMPRESSION OF A FROTHING MAD DOG EVERY TIME SOMEBODY WALKS BY.

THAT'S MY JOHN SUNUNU IMPRESSION.

WE HAVE TO APPROACH YOUR DATING PROBLEM LOGICALLY.

WE'LL BEGIN BY WRITING DOWN ALL OF THE QUALITIES YOU WANT IN A GIRLFRIEND.

MUCH LATER...

...AND SHE MUST BE A BALLERINA.

MY PAW IS CRAMPING.

OUR C E O IS ANNOUNCING A TEN-PERCENT STAFF REDUCTION TO CUT EXPENSES.

QUESTION: DIDN'T OUR C E O GET PAID TWENTY MILLION DOLLARS THIS YEAR?

YES...

BUT RISKY JOBS DESERVE HIGHER PAY.

QUESTION: DIDN'T YOU SAY WE WERE GETTING CUT?

THE STAFF CUTS WILL BE DETERMINED BY TOSSING A DART AT THE ORGANIZATION CHART WHILE BLINDFOLDED.

AAEEEE!

YOU SLAYED JOHNSON!

BOY, TALK ABOUT DECISIVE MANAGEMENT!

WE'RE SORRY TO HEAR YOU'RE GETTING LAID OFF, BRUCE.

WE CALCULATED THAT IF TEN OF YOUR FRIENDS HERE TOOK TEN PERCENT PAY CUTS THEN THE COMPANY CAN KEEP YOU.

GOSH! YOU'D DO THAT FOR ME?

NO. WE'RE HERE TO LOOK AT YOUR OFFICE FURNITURE.

DILBERT

By Scott Adams

LOOK, DOGBERT-- A WALLET.

IT'S FULL OF MONEY.

WE'RE RICH!!

WE MUST RETURN IT TO ITS OWNER.

WE'RE HONEST!

HIS BUSINESS CARD SAYS "SAM GROOPER, RUTHLESS CRIMINAL."

LET'S HOPE "RUTHLESS" MEANS HE DIVORCED HIS WIFE NAMED RUTH.

MR. GROOPER, WE FOUND YOUR WALLET. NO REWARD IS EXPECTED.

HAND IT OVER. GIVE ME YOUR WALLET TOO. THEN SLAP YOURSELVES AROUND AND SCRAM.

WE'RE MORONS!

11-24

DOGBERT'S CONFIRMATION HEARING FOR THE SUPREME COURT

THE SENATOR HAS 34 SECONDS...

I WONDER WHAT WOULD HAPPEN IF YOU LET THEM TALK AS LONG AS THEY WANTED.

I'LL BET THEY'D STARVE TO DEATH.

BUT THERE'S PROBABLY A DOWNSIDE.

AT DOGBERT'S CONFIRMATION HEARING FOR THE SUPREME COURT...

MISTER RATBERT, YOU'VE BEEN CALLED AS A CHARACTER WITNESS.

THE NOMINEE ONCE CALLED ME A LITTLE HINEY...

NEWS 50¢

LIAR!

PROBABLY NUTS!!

MISTER DOGBERT, DO YOU REALIZE THAT IF CONFIRMED FOR THE SUPREME COURT...

IT WOULD BE IMPROPER TO PURSUE YOUR STATED GOAL OF CONQUERING THE WORLD AND ENSLAVING ALL HUMANS?

ZZZZ

YOU WITHDREW?

APPARENTLY THERE ARE ALL THESE "UNWRITTEN" RULES.

DILBERT, YOUR NEW CO-WORKER IS ZIMBU THE MONKEY.

ZIMBU LEARNED ENGLISH FROM THE ZOO KEEPERS IN A SPECIAL PROGRAM.

THIS MONKEY IS AN INSULT TO THE INTELLIGENCE OF THE OTHER WORKERS AND I!

OTHER WORKERS AND "ME," NOT "I"!

LOOK, ZIMBU, YOU MIGHT HAVE LEARNED LANGUAGE SKILLS AT THE ZOO, BUT IT TAKES MORE THAN THAT TO BE AN ENGINEER.

DILBERT, ZIMBU, LET'S HIT THE CAFETERIA FOR MORNING DONUTS.

OKAY, AFTER TEN A.M. IT TAKES MORE THAN LANGUAGE SKILLS TO BE AN ENGINEER.

NOT TODAY-- WE HAVE A STAFF MEETING.

IT'S TIME TO END THIS CHARADE, ZIMBU!

YOUR LANGUAGE SKILLS ARE SIMPLE ROTE BEHAVIOR. MONKEYS ARE INCAPABLE OF LOGIC AND REASONING.

HA! AND THAT PROGRAM YOU'RE WRITING --IT'S PROBABLY IN "BASIC."

DO YOU EVER WORK?

DILBERT

By Scott Adams

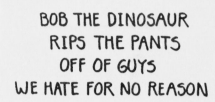

BOB THE DINOSAUR RIPS THE PANTS OFF OF GUYS WE HATE FOR NO REASON

YES!

GUYS WHO WEAR THOSE LITTLE HELMETS TO RIDE A BICYCLE.

DID A 100 "K" TODAY.

AAAAGH!!

SAFETY FIRST!

RIP

GUYS WHO KNOW ACTUAL DANCE STEPS.

WOMEN LOVE THAT STUFF!

AAAGH!!

GUYS WHO KNOW WINE.

FRUITY, YET TANNIC...

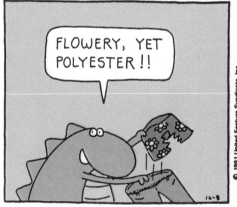

FLOWERY, YET POLYESTER!!

GUYS WHO CAN STOP A CONVERSATION COLD.

THAT REMINDS ME OF TRELLIS CODE MODULATION.

NOSTRADOGBERT PREDICTS THAT THE WORLD WILL END WITHIN A HUNDRED BILLION YEARS.

THAT'S A BIG RANGE.

(..)

WE IN THE BUSINESS CALL IT THE "GROSS PROPHET MARGIN."

OH YEAH, I'VE HEARD OF THAT.

WHEN'S THE BABY DUE?

BABY? WHAT BABY?

CAN'T A WOMAN GO OFF HER DIET FOR ONE DAY WITHOUT GETTING THAT QUESTION??

NEXT...

SO, WHEN'S THE BABY DUE?

KNOWLEDGE IS POWER, DOGBERT.

SOMEDAY, THE PEOPLE WHO KNOW HOW TO USE COMPUTERS WILL RULE OVER THOSE WHO DON'T.

AND THEY WILL HAVE A SPECIAL NAME FOR US.

SECRETARIES.

DILBERT

By Scott Adams

DILBERT
By Scott Adams

'TWAS THE NIGHT BEFORE CHRISTMAS...

WHEN A DUCK HIT THE SLED...

SMACK

SANTA FELL OUT...

AND DROPPED ON HIS HEAD...

HE WAS BARELY ALIVE, THIS JOLLY OLD ELF...

'TWAS THE HOLIDAY SEASON, SO I THOUGHT OF MYSELF...

HEY! I DON'T SEE ANY GIFTS HERE!

SO I STOLE HIS HAT AND BURIED HIM IN THE BACK YARD. THE END.

UH...THIS IS INTERESTING, DOGBERT.

THE SEQUEL IS TITLED "ELF WARS: THE TASTE OF VENISON."

12-22

WHAT DID YOU MEAN WHEN YOU SAID ALL EMPLOYEES ARE EMPOWERED?

DOES THAT MEAN I CAN CONTROL MY OWN BUDGET, MAKE DECISIONS WITHOUT TWELVE LEVELS OF APPROVAL, AND TAKE CALCULATED RISKS ON MY OWN?

NO, IT'S JUST A WAY TO BLAME EMPLOYEES FOR NOT DOING THE THINGS WE TELL THEM NOT TO DO.

NO WONDER YOU NEEDED A NEW WORD.

I'M USING A NEW SYSTEM FOR EVALUATING MY DATES. I JUST CHECK OFF BOXES ON THIS CARD THROUGHOUT THE NIGHT.

THERE... I JUST DINGED YOU A POINT FOR THAT NERVOUS TWITCH.

WOULD YOU SAY YOUR HEAD IS MORE LIKE A BLOCK OR A BUCKET?

DO YOU EVER WONDER ABOUT THE MEANING OF LIFE, DOGBERT?

I USED TO.

BUT I LOOKED IT UP IN THE DICTIONARY UNDER "L" AND THERE IT WAS — THE MEANING OF LIFE.

IT WAS LESS THAN I EXPECTED.

DID YOU TRY THE THESAURUS?

DILBERT

By Scott Adams

I'VE BEEN ASKED TO BRIEF EVERYBODY ON THE COMPANY'S POLICY FOR PROTECTING SECRET INFORMATION.

ALL SECRET INFORMATION MUST BE LOCKED UP AT NIGHT.

OUR SECRETS COULD BE OF GREAT VALUE TO OUR COMPETITORS.

IN FACT, SOME COMPANIES TRY TO BUY THE SECRETS OF THEIR COMPETITORS.

JUST OUT OF CURIOSITY, HOW MUCH WOULD OUR COMPETITORS PAY FOR OUR SECRETS?

OH, I DUNNO... MAYBE SEVERAL TIMES YOUR ANNUAL SALARY.

I DON'T THINK THIS WAS SOME OF MY BEST WORK.

I SAY WE ELVES HAVE BEEN PUSHED AROUND TOO LONG!

LET'S USE OUR ELF MAGIC TO CONQUER THE WORLD!!

YEAH! ELF MAGIC!

C'MON, PICK A CARD — ANY CARD!! AND THIS TIME BE SERIOUS!!

I'LL TAKE THE FORTY-THREE OF CLUBS.

FEAR US, DOG! WE ELVES ARE MAGIC. WATCH THIS!

I THINK WE HAD THE DOG'S FEAR AND RESPECT... UNTIL THE BUNNY MADE KARL EAT A BUG.

THE HUMANS ARE NOT AFRAID OF OUR ELF MAGIC. WE MUST GAIN THEIR RESPECT THROUGH VERBAL INTIMIDATION.

HEY, BOZO! WE'RE TALKING TO YOU, CHUBBY!

DONUTS

AND THEN KARL SAYS "DO YOU THINK YOU'RE GOING TO EAT ALL OF THOSE DONUTS?"

SHUT UP

DILBERT

By Scott Adams

THANKS FOR AGREEING TO BABY-SIT, DOGBERT.

NO SWEAT.

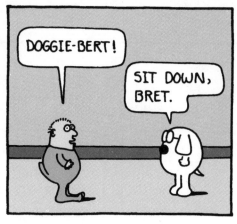

DOGGIE-BERT!

SIT DOWN, BRET.

YOU'RE IN YOUR MOST INNOCENT AND IMPRESSIONABLE YEARS.

AS AN ADULT, IT IS MY DUTY TO FILL YOUR SPONGE-LIKE BRAIN WITH INCREDIBLE NONSENSE FOR MY OWN ENTERTAINMENT.

YOUR PARENTS ARE REALLY SPACE ALIENS.

1-5-92

THEY'RE JUST FATTENING YOU UP SO THEY CAN EAT YOU!

THE SLAUGHTER-HOUSE IS A PLACE THEY CALL KINDERGARTEN!!

THANKS, DOGBERT. DID YOU CHANGE HIM?

PROBABLY.

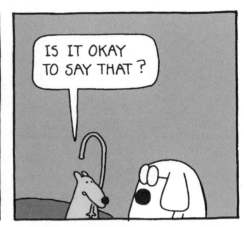

DILBERT

By Scott Adams

UNCLE NED, CAN WE SEE YOUR HUNTING TROPHIES AFTER DINNER?

OOOH...

I BAGGED THIS ONE AT THE ZOO.

THE ZOO? THAT'S ILLEGAL.

NO WONDER EVERYBODY GOT SO EXCITED.

THESE ARE SOME DOVES I KILLED WITH HELP FROM MY LOYAL DOG, RUSTY.

THAT'S RUSTY.

WE RAN OUT OF DOVES...

THESE WERE MY NEIGHBORS — FLORENCE, DAVE AND MUFFIN.

HEY, LOOK AT THE TIME! GOT TO RUN!

DON'T YOU WANT TO SEE MY "HALL-O'-POSTAL EMPLOYEES"?

NEW RULE: FIND OUT THEIR HOBBIES BEFORE YOU EAT THEIR POT ROAST.

WE SHOULD HAVE STAYED FOR THE "HALL-O'-POSTAL EMPLOYEES."

S. Adams

1-19

I THOUGHT YOU WERE MY FRIEND, RATBERT. WHY DID YOU TIP OFF THE AUTHORITIES ABOUT MY INSIDER STOCK TRADING?

I WAS AFRAID THAT IF YOU KEPT THE MONEY YOU WOULD LEAVE AND I'D NEVER SEE YOU AGAIN.

REALLY? GEE...

DID THEY GIVE YOU A REWARD?

YEAH, I'M OUTTA HERE!

I FIND YOU GUILTY OF STEALING MILLIONS IN AN INSIDER TRADING SCHEME.

LET'S SEE... ACCORDING TO MY SLIDING SCALE OF JUSTICE, THE PUNISHMENT AT YOUR INCOME IS... HMM...

I'M SENTENCED TO BE THE SUBJECT OF A KITTY KELLY BIOGRAPHY.

WHAT HAPPENED TO YOU?

KITTY KELLY WAS HERE TO WRITE YOUR BIOGRAPHY. SHE WAS ALL OVER ME. I THINK SHE TOOK MY WATCH.

I NEVER TRUST ANYBODY NAMED "KITTY."

I THINK I LOVE HER.

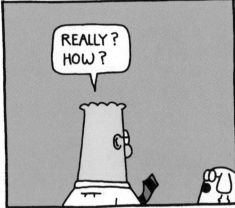

HOW'S THE NEW GUY DOING?

HE'S EXTREMELY PRODUCTIVE.

WE THINK HE'S ONE OF THOSE BUREAUCRACY SAVANTS.

I WAS SKEPTICAL ABOUT HIRING A DOG AS OUR NEW SQUARE-DANCE CALLER, BUT YOUR RESUMÉ IS IMPRESSIVE.

I DIDN'T EVEN KNOW YOU COULD WIN A PULITZER PRIZE FOR SQUARE-DANCE CALLING.

WOW! AND YOU'RE ALREADY IN THE ALBERDEEN HALL OF DUNG!

♫ SWING YOUR PARTNER, DOSEY-DO, NOW CLAP ♫ YOUR HANDS...

UH-OH, THAT'S ALL THE SQUARE DANCE MOVES I KNOW ... I'LL BLUFF THE REST.

SLAP YOUR PARTNER IN THE FACE, ♫ WRITE BAD CHECKS ALL OVER THE PLACE, ♫ FLIRT WITH STRANGERS, ANNOY YOUR SPOUSE, GET A DIVORCE AND LOSE YOUR HOUSE...UH...

DOSEY-DO

SINCE THIS IS THE FIRST TIME YOU'VE BEEN TO A MENSA MEETING, I'LL EXPLAIN A FEW THINGS.

WHEN THE MUSIC STOPS WE ALL LINK ARMS TO SIMULATE THE DNA STRUCTURE OF A FEATURED CELEBRITY.

TO BE HONEST, I THINK A LOT OF IT IS JUST RANDOM.

I JUST REALIZED THAT SOME CARBON MOLECULES MUST BE SHAPED LIKE HOLLOW GEODESIC BALLS!!

ERK!!!

THAT'S WHAT HAPPENS WHEN A FLASH OF INSIGHT HITS THE WRONG PLACE.

EVOLUTION MUST BE TRUE BECAUSE IT IS A LOGICAL CONCLUSION OF THE SCIENTIFIC METHOD.

BUT SCIENCE IS BASED ON THE IRRATIONAL BELIEF THAT BECAUSE WE CANNOT PERCEIVE REALITY ALL AT ONCE, THINGS CALLED "TIME" AND "CAUSE AND EFFECT" EXIST.

THAT'S WHAT I WAS TAUGHT AND THAT'S WHAT I BELIEVE.

SOUNDS CULTISH.

DILBERT

By Scott Adams

DILBERT! DOGBERT!

THANKS FOR INVITING US OVER.

WE THOUGHT YOU'D LIKE TO SEE OUR HOME VIDEO OF LITTLE TIMMY'S BIRTH.

WE CAPTURED EVERY BEAUTIFUL MOMENT ON VHS!

HAVE YOU EVER SEEN A CAESAREAN SECTION BEFORE?

THE DOCTOR IS MAKING THE INCISION!

NOW THEY'RE REMOVING THE SQUIGGLY THING!

WAIT... THIS MIGHT BE THE WRONG TAPE... I THINK THIS IS YOUR APPENDECTOMY VIDEO.

EITHER THAT OR LITTLE TIMMY ISN'T VERY PHOTOGENIC.

WHAT HAPPENED WITH THE ROBOT YOU WERE BUILDING?

NOBODY CAN MAKE A ROBOT. IT'S IMPOSSIBLE.

HMM... A PERFECTLY GOOD ROBOT. PROBABLY JUST NEEDS A NEURO-SPECTRUM FIELD CALIBRATION.

THAT WHOLE ROBOT PROJECT WAS BAD FOR MY EGO AS AN ENGINEER.

HEY! GUESS WHO'S WAY SMARTER THAN YOU!

REMEMBER, THE "ROBOT'S CODE" REQUIRES YOU TO USE YOUR VAST STRENGTH TO SERVE, PROTECT, AND NEVER HARM HUMANS.

HA! I DIDN'T SIGN ANY "ROBOT'S CODE." IN FACT, WITH MY VAST STRENGTH I CAN MAKE YOU SERVE ME!

I FORGOT TO PROGRAM IN THE "ROBOT'S CODE."

MAYBE I'LL CRUSH YOUR HEAD JUST FOR FUN!

I MADE SOME PANTS OUT OF THE CLOTHES IN YOUR DRESSER.

BAD ROBOT!! I WANT YOU TO TELL ME WHY WHAT YOU DID WAS WRONG.

IT'S NOT WRONG. I REMEMBERED TO MAKE UNDERPANTS OUT OF THE DRAPES.

OUR ROBOT IS TAUNTING DILBERT MERCILESSLY. IS THERE ANY WAY TO STOP HIM?

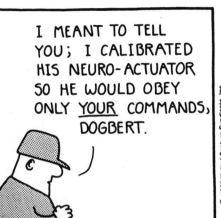

I MEANT TO TELL YOU; I CALIBRATED HIS NEURO-ACTUATOR SO HE WOULD OBEY ONLY YOUR COMMANDS, DOGBERT.

WHAT DID HE SAY?

HE SAYS THERE'S NOTHING YOU CAN DO.

WE NEED TO DO SOMETHING ABOUT YOUR TOTAL LACK OF ETHICS AND SOCIAL CONSCIENCE.

I HAD DILBERT BUILD THIS GUILT MODULE FOR YOUR CONTROL BOARD. IT HAS THE SYNTHESIZED SHAME OF EVERY MAJOR BELIEF SYSTEM.

LATER

FRANKLY, I LIKED HIM BETTER BEFORE.

I AM UNWORTHY TO ROLL IN YOUR SPITTLE.

I WORRY... IS IT MY FAULT THAT PEOPLE GET HEART ATTACKS?

NO... THAT'S FROM EATING TOO MANY COWS.

IS THE CALIFORNIA DROUGHT MY FAULT?

NO... THAT'S FROM WATER SUBSIDIES TO COWS.

GLOBAL WARMING?

COWS AGAIN.

COWS ARE DESTROYING THE EARTH?

THEY'RE BETTER ORGANIZED THAN YOU'D THINK.

WE NEED A NAME FOR YOU.

I DON'T DESERVE A NAME.

EVERYTHING THAT'S WRONG WITH THE WORLD IS MY FAULT. I RUE THE DAY I WAS CREATED.

I NAME YOU "RUEBERT."

AAAGH! PEOPLE WILL SPELL IT WRONG AND IT'S MY FAULT!!

WHAT ARE YOU DOING IN MY LAB, RUEBERT?

I AM CREATING A FEMININE ROBOT TO NURTURE AND SERVE ME.

I DIDN'T KNOW HOW TO PROGRAM IT, SO I FOUND THIS "NATIONAL ORGANIZATION OF WOMEN" IN THE PHONE BOOK...

IT TURNS OUT THAT THIS IS EXACTLY THE KIND OF THING THEY LIKE TO HELP WITH.

DO YOU LIKE SURPRISES?

MY MATE IS COMPLETE! I WILL NOW HAVE EONS OF MARITAL BLISS!

I DON'T THINK SO, GOMER. I'M GOING TO SHOP AROUND... MAYBE FIND SOMEBODY MORE ENLIGHTENED THAN A CAN OPENER.

IT'S RUEBERT, NOT GOMER, AND I'M THE ONLY OTHER ROBOT IN EXISTENCE!

I'M IN HELL.

DILBERT

By Scott Adams

BANK OF ETHEL

NOW A SECRET SWISS BANK

I'D LIKE TO WITHDRAW TWO HUNDRED DOLLARS.

WHAT'S YOUR SECRET SWISS ACCOUNT NUMBER?

I DON'T HAVE A SECRET ACCOUNT. IT'S JUST A REGULAR ACCOUNT.

WRONG. I CHANGED ALL OF THE ACCOUNTS INTO SECRET SWISS ACCOUNTS.

OH, OKAY, WHAT'S MY SECRET ACCOUNT NUMBER?

IT'S A SECRET.

THEN HOW DO I GET MY MONEY OUT?

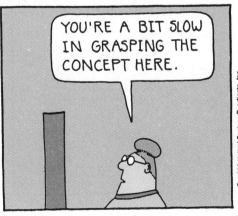

YOU'RE A BIT SLOW IN GRASPING THE CONCEPT HERE.

OKAY, OKAY I'LL JUST OPEN A NEW ACCOUNT.

DO YOU HAVE ANY PREVIOUS BANKING REFERENCES?

RATBERT, I'M LOOKING FOR A VICE PRESIDENT FOR MY TICKET.

I NEED SOMEBODY WHO IS SO INEPT AND SIMPLE-MINDED THAT I ALWAYS LOOK GOOD IN COMPARISON.

I DON'T UNDERSTAND.

OKAY, OKAY, YOU'VE GOT THE JOB.

SURE, DOGBERT, I'LL BE YOUR ELECTION CAMPAIGN STRATEGIST.

YOU CAN WIN IF YOU PROMISE TO SELL OUR NATIONAL PARKS TO FOREIGNERS AND SHARE THE PROFITS.

I COULDN'T DO THAT.

YOU COULDN'T SELL THE PARKS?

I COULDN'T SHARE THE PROFITS.

THE KEY TO WINNING THE ELECTION IS VOTER TURNOUT.

TO BE SPECIFIC, YOU WANT EVERYBODY TO STAY HOME EXCEPT YOU.

I'VE WORKED UP A LITTLE AD CAMPAIGN.

HE TOUCHED THE VOTING BOOTH BEFORE YOU DID.

AND HE NEVER WASHES HIS HANDS

DILBERT

By Scott Adams

DOGBERT PRESENTS

THE SEVEN ADVANTAGES OF BEING DUMB

#1. IMPENDING DOOM DOESN'T BOTHER YOU

THERE'S A HOLE IN THE OZONE LAYER.

COOL!

#2. TELEVISION IS A SOURCE OF CONSTANT WONDER

I WONDER IF DOOGIE IS A DOCTOR IN REAL LIFE.

#3. YOU HAVE A SOLUTION FOR EVERY PROBLEM

IF PEOPLE ARE STARVING IN AFRICA THEY SHOULD MOVE TO FRANCE.

#4. YOU ARE NOT CONSTRAINED BY A BUDGET

IT WAS FREE! THEY JUST MAKE YOU SIGN PAPERS!

#5. YOU'VE SEEN ELVIS. FREQUENTLY.

IT'S THE KING!

#6. INSTANT REPLAYS ARE AS EXCITING AS LIVE ACTION.

THIS TIME HE COULD MAKE IT.

#7. YOU RECEIVE TWICE AS MANY COMPLIMENTS.

YOU'RE KIND OF THE DAN QUAYLE OF DINOSAURS.

REALLY?! WOW!

3-1

THE POLL RESULTS ARE IN.

YOU STILL HAVE LOW NAME-RECOGNITION OUTSIDE OF THE LIVING ROOM... BUT SOME GUY IN THE KITCHEN THINKS HE'S HEARD OF YOU.

DON'T BE DISCOURAGED, UH...UH...

DOGBERT!

I'M GOING TO HOST MY OWN TELEVISION SHOW.

IT'S CALLED "DOGBERT'S WORLD OF AMAZINGLY IGNORANT PEOPLE."

OF COURSE, I'LL FILM YOU IN SHADOWS AND ALTER YOUR VOICE ELECTRON-ICALLY.

THAT'S VERY CONSIDERATE.

WELCOME TO DOGBERT'S WORLD OF AMAZINGLY IGNORANT PEOPLE.

TONIGHT WE'LL VISIT PEOPLE WHO DON'T UNDERSTAND ECONOMICS BUT TALK ABOUT IT ANYWAY.

SO, I HEARD THE FED INCREASED THE MONEY SUPPLY, BUT I CHECKED MY BANK BALANCE AND IT'S THE SAME AS BEFORE.

THAT ISN'T FAIR.

ON THIS EPISODE OF "DOGBERT'S AMAZINGLY IGNORANT PEOPLE" WE ASK PEOPLE TO FIND AUSTRALIA ON THE GLOBE.

3-5

IS THAT THE PLACE WITH THE ALPS OR THE KANGAROOS?

I THINK IT'S IN LONDON.

WHEN WE RETURN: INSPIRATION BECOMES BITTER DISAPPOINTMENT.

HEY! WHO SAYS IT HAS TO BE ON THE OUTSIDE?

© 1992 United Feature Syndicate, Inc.

ON TODAY'S EPISODE OF "DOGBERT'S AMAZINGLY IGNORANT PEOPLE" WE TALK TO PEOPLE WHO DON'T KNOW HISTORY.

HOW MANY PEOPLE PERISHED BECAUSE OF WORLD WAR II?

UH... 400?

© 1992 United Feature Syndicate, Inc.

THE ANSWER IS FIFTY MILLION.

OH... ROUNDING.

3-6

WHAT PRODUCT ARE WE TESTING TODAY, DOC?

3-7

WE'LL BE TESTING THE SAFETY OF COSMETICS. THIS WILL BE YOUR MOST DANGEROUS ASSIGNMENT.

© 1992 United Feature Syndicate, Inc.

SOMETIMES I HATE THIS JOB.

HEY BABY!!

WHOA!! WHOA!!

DOGBERT SUES DILBERT FOR PETIMONY.

I CALL RATBERT AS MY FIRST WITNESS.

3-12

IS IT TRUE THAT DILBERT IS A SECRET CAT LOVER WHO OFTEN BETRAYED THE TRUST OF HIS FAITHFUL DOG?

IT'S TRUE.

I OFTEN FOUND HIM ALONE DRINKING ROOT BEER AND READING "CAT FANCY" MAGAZINE IN HIS UNDERWEAR... IT'S A SICKNESS.

AT THE PETIMONY TRIAL

YOUR HONOR, I REQUEST THAT DOGBERT'S SUIT AGAINST ME BE DROPPED...

3-13

...ON THE GROUNDS THAT THERE'S NO HABEUS CORPUS, NO LO CONTENDRE, AND NO E PLURIBUS UNUM.

WITH LUCK, HE DOESN'T KNOW LATIN EITHER.

BAILIFF, CLUB THIS MAN.

DOGBERT SUES DILBERT FOR PETIMONY

THE DEFENSE CALLS FUZZY THE CAT.

3-14

ISN'T IT TRUE THAT I DID NOT IN FACT PET YOU, BUT ONLY PUSHED YOU AWAY IN MILD DISGUST WHEN YOU RUBBED MY LEG?

I HAVE THIS SUDDEN URGE TO BURY YOU IN PINE-SCENTED SAND.

MISTER DOGBERT, YOU MADE A GOOD ARGUMENT IN YOUR PETIMONY SUIT AGAINST DILBERT...

BUT DILBERT HAD SOME GOOD POINTS, TOO... I CALL IT A TIE.

THIRD TIE THIS WEEK... MAYBE IT'S ME...

I'M NOT REALLY A GENIUS.

DID YOU SAY SOMETHING?

I'M PRACTICING MY FALSE HUMILITY.

IS THIS JUST A WAY TO WEASEL MORE COMPLIMENTS OUT OF PEOPLE?

OH, I COULD NEVER BE THAT CLEVER.

I'VE BEEN USING FALSE HUMILITY TO WEASEL COMPLIMENTS OUT OF PEOPLE...

BUT I KNOW YOU'RE WAY TOO SMART TO FALL FOR THAT TRICK, RATBERT.

ACTUALLY, I'M AS DUMB AS TOAST.

THEN I FOUND I COULD USE FALSE COMPLIMENTS TO MAKE PEOPLE INSULT THEMSELVES.

IT'S EASY TO MAKE INSECURE PEOPLE INSULT THEMSELVES.

GOOD MORNING, MA'AM. YOU LOOK THIN AND SEXY TODAY!

SEXY?! HA! I'M A WHALE ... A WHALE WITH A BAD HAIRDO!

NEXT

UH... DILBERT, ABOUT THAT ASSIGNMENT I GAVE YOU LAST MONTH...

REMEMBER HOW YOU THOUGHT IT WAS A SILLY AND RIDICULOUS ASSIGNMENT?

YEAH?

WELL, IT TURNS OUT THAT I'VE BEEN SPONTANEOUSLY CHANNELING THE SPIRIT OF BOZO THE CLOWN.

I BOUGHT SOME "SMART PILLS" FOR YOU. THEY'RE MADE FROM CHINESE HERBS.

I SAW A NEWS STORY ABOUT THESE... AND NATURALLY I THOUGHT OF YOU.

I'VE DISCOVERED THE PERFECT GIFT ITEM.

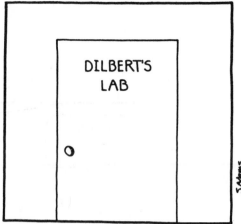

DILBERT'S LAB

ANY LUCK WITH YOUR HAIR GROWTH FORMULA?

DEFINE "LUCK."

THE GOOD NEWS IS THAT MY HAIR GROWTH FORMULA WORKS.

IN RETROSPECT, I SHOULD HAVE TESTED IT ON MY SCALP INSTEAD OF RUBBING IT ALL OVER MY BODY.

HINDSIGHT...

YEAH...

THINGS HAVE BEEN STRANGE SINCE THE MISHAP WITH MY HAIR GROWTH FORMULA.

I HAVE A STRONG URGE TO BUY SUN-GLASSES AND DRIVE A PORSCHE...

AND I WORRY THAT PEOPLE WON'T TAKE ME SERIOUSLY.

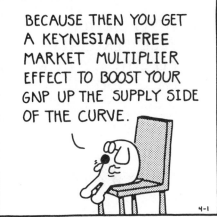

THE CANINE TAX REBATE BILL WAS PASSED BY CONGRESS TODAY.

THE BILL'S AUTHOR, MISTER DOGBERT, SUCCESSFULLY PINNED THE LABEL "DOG KICKING LIBERAL" ON ALL WHO OPPOSED HIM.

WAS THAT ETHICAL?

THA-A-AT'S IT. YOU'RE ON THE LIST.

...SO, THEN I THOUGHT, HA! MAYBE THERE'S A BUG IN THE COMPILER PROGRAM ITSELF!

AAAGH!

MAYBE THAT STORY WENT ON A LITTLE LONG...

WHAT GAVE IT AWAY?

HAVE YOU HEARD ABOUT THE IDAHO FLU THAT'S GOING AROUND?

AT FIRST YOU FEEL PERFECTLY HEALTHY... THEN BAM, YOU DIE.

HEY, I FEEL PERFECTLY HEALTHY RIGHT NOW.

MY WORK HERE IS DONE.

DILBERT

By Scott Adams

I'M OFF TO MY NEW JOB AS AN MTV REPORTER.

RAP STAR FRESHY Q, WHAT IS THE KEY TO YOUR SUCCESS?

ALWAYS BE YOURSELF. DON'T FOLLOW THE CROWD. BE TRUE TO YOUR INSTINCTS.

DID YOU INVENT RAP?

UH... NO.

OH, BUT YOU PROBABLY PIONEERED THIS STYLE OF DRESSING.

NOT EXACTLY.

BUT YOU WRITE ALL OF YOUR OWN MUSIC.

NO... I BUY IT.

THE DANCE STEPS?

I HIRE A CHOREO-GRAPHER.

WELL, I'LL BET NOBODY ELSE FOLDS HIS ARMS QUITE LIKE YOU.

I DON'T LIKE THE DIREC-TION THIS IS HEADING.

© 1992 United Feature Syndicate, Inc.

4-5

DILBERT, I'M PUTTING YOU ON A ROTATIONAL ASSIGNMENT...

YOU WILL BE WORKING IN MARKETING UNTIL FURTHER NOTICE.

MARKETING
TWO DRINK MINIMUM

DILBERT IS TRANSFERRED TO MARKETING

YOU LOOK LOST.

I NEVER KNEW THAT MARKETING WAS LIKE THIS ... DO YOU PEOPLE DO ANY WORK?

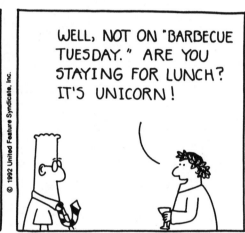

WELL, NOT ON "BARBECUE TUESDAY." ARE YOU STAYING FOR LUNCH? IT'S UNICORN!

DILBERT IS TRANSFERRED TO MARKETING

EVERY TUESDAY WE BARBECUE A UNICORN.

MAKE MINE RARE. HA HA! GET IT? RARE?

I'M NOT SURE I BELIEVE THIS IS THE "BEST PART."

DILBERT

By Scott Adams

DOGBERT'S GUIDE
TO MOVIE
ADVERTISEMENTS

TRUST ME.

"THUMBS UP."

GENE SISKEL

MEANING: ROGER EBERT HATES IT.

"NOMINATED FOR AN ACADEMY AWARD."

NOTICE THEY DON'T SAY FOR WHAT -- PROBABLY "BEST GAFFER."

"FUNNIEST MOVIE OF THE YEAR."

HE SAW IT IN MID-JANUARY.

"☆☆☆☆ ... A MASTER-PIECE!"

THE MOVIE STUDIO ONLY PAID OFF ONE CRITIC. MUST BE A LOW-BUDGET FILM.

"POWERFUL PERFORMANCES."

IT'S A DOWNER. SOMEBODY PROBABLY GETS A DISEASE AND LOSES THE FARM.

S. Adams

4-12

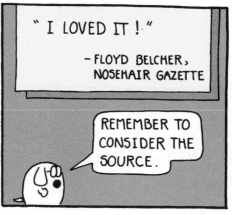

"I LOVED IT!"

-FLOYD BELCHER, NOSEHAIR GAZETTE

REMEMBER TO CONSIDER THE SOURCE.

"STALLONE'S FUNNIEST MOVIE YET."

I THINK YOU GET THE HANG OF IT.

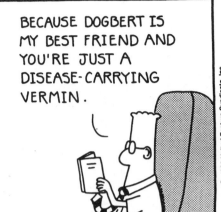

DILBERT

By Scott Adams

DOGBERT, COME LOOK AT OUR NEW CAR!

IT HAS ALL OF THE MOST IMPORTANT SAFETY FEATURES.

YOU GOT YOUR ANTI-LOCK BRAKES, YOUR REINFORCED BUMPERS, YOUR AUTOMATIC SEATBELTS AND YOUR DRIVER-SIDE AIR BAG.

I DIDN'T HEAR "PASSENGER SIDE AIR BAG" IN THAT LIST

IT TURNS OUT THAT IT'S ONLY ECONOMICAL TO SAVE THE PERSON WHO MAKES THE BUYING DECISION.

4-19

BUT I GOT A BABY SEAT IN CASE YOU WANT TO USE THAT.

WELL, THANK YOU FOR LETTING ME CHOOSE BETWEEN HUMILIATION AND DEATH.

I'VE GOT A BETTER IDEA.

OOH... JUST WAIT UNTIL MY TURN.

WATCH ME RAM THAT COP CAR.

153

DILBERT

By Scott Adams

I WILL LISTEN TO YOUR SAD STORY $5.00

I HAVE A SAD STORY.

SIT DOWN.

I WAS A WORLD RENOWNED MONKEY TRAINER.

I HAD IT ALL: FAME, MONEY, BEAUTIFUL FAMILY.

THEN I DISCOVERED THAT THE MONKEYS WERE PLOTTING AGAINST ME.

THEY EMBEZZLED ALL OF MY MONEY AND KIDNAPPED MY WIFE.

THEN MY WIFE FELL IN LOVE WITH THEIR LEADER, BING-BONG.

HA HA HA!

WERE YOU LAUGHING?

HERE'S MY FIVE BUCKS. THANKS.

© 1992 United Feature Syndicate, Inc.

DILBERT

By Scott Adams

HOW CAN I TELL WHEN SPAGHETTI IS COOKED?

I'LL HAVE TO WEAR THE HAT TO ANSWER THAT QUESTION.

THE SPAGHETTI IS DONE WHEN YOU CAN THROW IT AT THE WALL AND MAKE IT STICK.

SEEMS ODD... BUT HE WAS WEARING THE HAT.

WHAP! SPLASH!

PREFERABLY, ONE STRAND AT A TIME.

TONIGHT ON "LARRY KING LIVE" WE HAVE A DOG WHO MAKES SEXY BEER COMMERCIALS, PLUS AN ANGRY FEMINIST.

5-14

HIS COMMERCIALS ENCOURAGE DISCRIMINATION AGAINST WOMEN BY PORTRAYING US ALL AS SEX OBJECTS.

ARE YOU SAYING MEN ARE SO DUMB, THEY GET THEIR VIEWS ON LIFE FROM BEER COMMERCIALS?

I CALL THEM LIKE I SEE THEM.

HEY, THAT'S A GOOD TECHNIQUE: COMBING YOUR EAR HAIR OVER THE BALD SPOT!

I'VE BEEN WORKING ON THE EYEBROWS-COMBED-OVER-THE-HEAD METHOD.

5-15

SOMEBODY SHOULD TALK TO THAT MAN.

I'M FEELING CONFIDENT TODAY WITH WHAT APPEARS TO BE A FULL HEAD OF HAIR.

NOBODY SUSPECTS THAT I'M ACTUALLY COMBING THE HAIR THAT GROWS IN MY EARS OVER THE TOP OF MY OTHERWISE BALD HEAD.

5-16

IT'S AMAZING HOW CLUELESS THESE PEOPLE ARE.

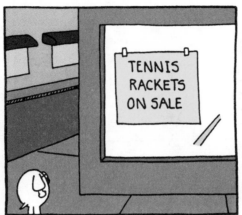

I NEED AN OUTSIDE CONSULTANT LIKE YOU TO HELP WITH LAY-OFFS.

MY MAIN CONCERN IS TO MINIMIZE THE PAIN AND HARDSHIP THAT GOES WITH THIS.

WITH GENEROUS SEVERANCE PAY?

NO, I THINK THAT WOULD ONLY MAKE MY PAIN AND SUFFERING WORSE.

5-28

AS YOUR CONSULTANT, I RECOMMEND THE "CAN-O-MATIC" TO REDUCE STAFF LEVELS.

DISGUISED AS A RESTROOM STALL, THE CAN-O-MATIC RANDOMLY FIRES PEOPLE BY SLAPPING A PINK SLIP ON THEIR BACKS AND CATAPULTING THEM OUT OF THE BUILDING.

5-29

BUT I WON'T GET TO SEE THE EXPRESSIONS ON THEIR FACES.

WELL, WE COULD FLING THEM PAST THE SECURITY CAMERAS HERE...

MY CONSULTANT ADVISED ME TO HANDLE THE LAY-OFFS IN A DIRECT, PROFESSIONAL WAY.

SO, THROUGHOUT THE DAY I'LL BE SNEAKING UP ON PEOPLE AND STAMPING "CANCELLED" ON THEIR BACKS.

5-30

LET ME SEE IF I UNDERSTAND...

HEY! IS THAT THE GOODYEAR BLIMP?

DILBERT

By Scott Adams

THANKS FOR YOUR TIME, DILBERT. IT'S ALWAYS GOOD TO GET THE TECHNICAL PERSPECTIVE.

HEY, IT'S LUNCHTIME. WOULD YOU LIKE TO JOIN ME IN THE CAFETERIA?

OOH... NO, I COULDN'T DO THAT.

I'M ON THE MANAGEMENT TRACK, SO I CAN'T BE SEEN EATING LUNCH WITH YOU.

IF I'M SEEN WITH AN ORDINARY EMPLOYEE THEN PEOPLE WILL THINK I'M ORDINARY.

I'D LIKE TO EAT WITH THE SENIOR EXECUTIVES, BUT OF COURSE THEY DON'T WANT TO BE SEEN WITH ME.

SO I'VE PERFECTED A METHOD OF SLIPPING QUIETLY AWAY AT LUNCH TIME.

THE SCARY PART IS THAT SOMEDAY THAT MAN WILL BE MY BOSS.

5-31

NOBODY EVER CALLS ON MY NEW VIDEO PHONE SO I ROUTED THE TELEVISION SIGNAL TO IT.

NOW I CAN PRETEND THAT CELEBRITIES ARE CALLING ME ALL DAY.

OOH... DOLLY PARTON IS CALLING. I'LL BET IT'S FOR ME AGAIN.

ALL WEEK I'VE BEEN WATCHING VIOLENT MOVIES AT THE LAB.

A GROUP OF PARENTS ARE STUDYING ME TO SEE IF I BECOME INURED TO VIOLENCE.

ARE YOU?

YEAH. I'M PLANNING TO GNAW THE PARENTS TO DEATH TOMORROW.

I DON'T KNOW WHAT WE CAN DO TO MEET MORE MEN.

HI, MY NAME IS DILBERT.

GET LOST... I'M ARMED.

AND THE MEN WE DO MEET ALL HAVE THAT SAME STUNNED BUNNY LOOK.

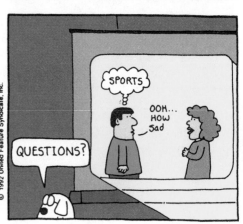

DILBERT

By Scott Adams

DOGBERT'S CONFESS-O-RAMA

EMPLOYEES ONLY   SINNERS

DOGBERT, I HAVE SINNED.

I WAS GOING TO MAKE CHOCOLATE CHIP COOKIES...

BUT I MADE THE MISTAKE OF TASTING A CHOCOLATE CHIP RIGHT FROM THE BAG.

BEFORE I KNEW IT, I HAD SCARFED THE ENTIRE BAG OF CHIPS!

FOR PENANCE YOU MUST MAKE A LITTLE DUNCE HAT FROM OLD "CATHY" COMIC STRIPS...

THEN WEAR THE LITTLE HAT WHILE DANCING NAKED ON YOUR LAWN WITH THE SPRINKLERS ON.

THANK YOU, DOGBERT.

© 1992 United Feature Syndicate, Inc.

6-14

IT'S SO REWARDING TO BE ABLE TO GIVE SOMETHING BACK TO THE COMMUNITY.

I'M PROUD TO ANNOUNCE THAT THE COMPANY HAS FOUND YET ANOTHER WAY TO DEHUMANIZE THE EMPLOYEES.

FROM NOW ON YOU WILL WEAR IDENTIFICATION BADGES AT WORK. THIS SYMBOLIZES THAT PEOPLE WHO LOOK LIKE YOU ARE OFTEN CRIMINALS.

OH... AND THE CAFETERIA IS CLOSED. WE'LL JUST LAY DOWN SOME ALFALFA IN THE BREAK ROOM.

MAYBE TED CAN ANSWER THAT QUESTION...

UH-OH

THEY'RE TRYING TO MAKE ME WORK. I'LL HAVE TO USE BODY LANGUAGE TO DISCOURAGE THEM.

UH... NEVER MIND

IT'S WORKING.

I'D LIKE TO APPLY FOR A "BANK OF ETHEL" CREDIT CARD.

SIT DOWN AND SHUT UP.

IT'S 21% INTEREST PLUS SURPRISINGLY HIGH ANNUAL FEES. WE'LL DO A CREDIT CHECK AND A FULL BODY CAVITY SEARCH.

...AND I HAD TO SMILE THE WHOLE TIME BECAUSE THEY WERE FILMING IT FOR THEIR TELEVISION ADS.

YOU HAVE TO ADMIRE THEIR ATTITUDE.

DILBERT

By Scott Adams

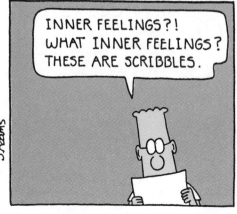

TELL ME WHAT YOU'VE ACCOMPLISHED THIS YEAR SO I CAN WRITE YOUR PERFORMANCE APPRAISAL

THE INVENTIONS I MADE LAST YEAR —— THAT YOU THOUGHT WERE WORTHLESS, WILL GENERATE TWELVE MILLION IN LICENSE FEES NEXT YEAR!

SO, NO REAL ACCOMPLISHMENTS THIS YEAR?

I'M GOING TO OPEN A SCHOOL FOR PEOPLE WITH NO COMMON SENSE.

WHO WOULD PAY TO GO TO A SCHOOL THAT TEACHES SOMETHING THAT CAN'T BE LEARNED?

EXCEPT MAYBE PEOPLE WITH NO COMMON SENSE...

BINGO.

WELCOME TO DOGBERT'S SCHOOL OF COMMON SENSE.

I'VE ASKED YOU TO PAY TUITION IN ADVANCE; THAT WAY IF YOU'RE UNSATISFIED WITH THE SCHOOL, YOU'LL HAVE THE ADDED NEGOTIATING LEVERAGE OF HAVING ALREADY PAID.

AND THANKS, ALICE, FOR ASKING IF TIPPING IS CUSTOMARY.

DOGBERT'S SCHOOL OF COMMON SENSE.

WHO CAN SHOW ME HOW TO GET THE WATER OUT OF THIS BOOT?

IF YOU HAVE TROUBLE, THE DIRECTIONS ARE WRITTEN ON THE HEEL.

I'M SORRY, BETTY. I CAN ONLY GIVE YOU PARTIAL CREDIT FOR TRYING TO ABSORB THE LIQUID WITH YOUR HAIR.

DOGBERT'S SCHOOL OF COMMON SENSE.

TODD, SHOW THE CLASS HOW YOU HAND THESE SCISSORS TO RUSSELL.

DON'T RUN! DON'T RUN!

AAAGH!

SORRY, RUSSELL. IT'S THE TEACHER'S FAULT; HE DIDN'T EVEN ASK IF I NEED LEFT-HANDED SCISSORS.

DOGBERT'S SCHOOL OF COMMON SENSE

THIS IS THE STORY OF CLAYTON THE AUTO MECHANIC.

CLAYTON SMOKED CIGARS WHILE WORKING ON GASOLINE ENGINES. WHAT PROBLEM DID THIS CAUSE?

BOOM

HE WAS HIT BY LIGHTNING EVERY TIME?

DOES ANYBODY BESIDE CLAYTON HAVE A GUESS?

DILBERT
By Scott Adams

I'M GOING TO START JOGGING AGAIN.

WHY DOES EVERYBODY TIE THEIR LACES IN THE SAME TYPE OF KNOT?

FROM AN ENGINEERING PERSPECTIVE, THERE ARE PLENTY OF GOOD ALTERNATIVES TO THE STANDARD KNOT.

THIS IS HOW INNOVATION BEGINS; ONE MAN WHO REFUSES TO ACCEPT THE CONVENTIONAL WISDOM.

HA HA! I'LL INVENT MY OWN KNOT! A REBELLIOUS, AUDACIOUS KNOT!

LIKE THIS AND THIS AND THIS! HA HA HA!!

MANY PEOPLE WONDER WHY THERE HAVEN'T BEEN MORE ENGINEERS IN THE OLYMPICS.

CALL THE BOY SCOUTS.

THIS WILL BE OUR MOST MEMORABLE VACATION YET.

... AND IN THE EVENT OF A SNOWY MOUNTAINSIDE CRASH, THE YOUNG AND FEEBLE PASSENGERS ARE COMPLETELY EDIBLE.

BUT CAPTAIN BOB PROMISES HE WON'T MAKE THAT MISTAKE AGAIN.

WE'RE ALIVE... WE MUST HAVE BEEN THROWN CLEAR WHEN THE JET HIT THE MOUNTAIN

I'M CAPTAIN BOB. SORRY ABOUT THE CRASH. WHAT ARE THE ODDS I'D HIT THIS SAME MOUNTAIN ON EVERY FLIGHT?

WE'RE IN LUCK. CAPTAIN BOB KNOWS HOW TO SURVIVE THESE SITUATIONS.

NICE FOLKS. I'LL EAT THEM LAST.

I'VE SURVIVED SEVERAL JET CRASHES THIS YEAR, SO LISTEN TO ME.

THE BEST WAY TO PREVENT FROSTBITE IS TO RUB WORCESTERSHIRE SAUCE ON YOUR BODY AND WHACK YOURSELF REPEATEDLY WITH A MEAT TENDERIZER.

I WONDER WHY HE HAD ENOUGH OF THESE FOR EVERYBODY?

WHACK WHACK

CAPTAIN BOB, I THINK YOU'RE PLANNING TO EAT THE OTHER SURVIVORS.

HA HA! TOO BAD YOUR ONLY HOPE IS TO SEND A MESSAGE TO THE VILLAGE AT THE BASE OF THIS MOUNTAIN.

7-2

WHEN YOU ROLL INTO TOWN, TELL THEM DOGBERT SENT YOU.

WHAP!

ZING

© 1992 United Feature Syndicate. Inc.

LUCKY AIRLINES? I DEMAND PAYMENT FOR THE LUGGAGE I LOST WHEN WE CRASHED INTO THE MOUNTAIN.

7-3

NO, TECHNICALLY IT'S NOT "LOST." . . . WELL, YES, I DID EAT YOUR COMPLIMENTARY PEANUTS . . .

© 1992 United Feature Syndicate. Inc.

HELP ME OUT HERE . . . SO FAR, I'VE AGREED TO HOT-WAX THEIR TARMAC.

EVERYBODY IN THE OFFICE GETS A TURN HOLDING MY NEW BABY.

NEXT.

UH-OH . . . SNEEZE COMING.

© 1992 United Feature Syndicate. Inc.

ACHOOO

OOH! LOOK WHAT HE DOES WHEN YOU SNEEZE ON HIM.

HE LOOKS LIKE A PRUNE!

7-4

DILBERT

By Scott Adams

DILBERT, DO YOU HAVE A MINUTE?

THE COMPANY IS DOING A SURVEY OF EMPLOYEE ATTITUDES ABOUT THEIR BOSSES.

IT'S TOTALLY ANONYMOUS, SO YOU DON'T HAVE TO FEAR ANY RETRIBUTION.

OOPS! IT LOOKS LIKE YOUR QUESTIONAIRE IS A BIT DOG-EARED.

I'LL PUT MY PHONE NUMBER ON THE CONFIDENTIAL ENVELOPE IN CASE YOU NEED ME.

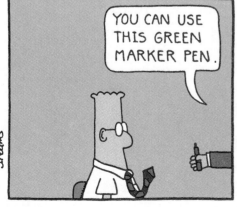

YOU CAN USE THIS GREEN MARKER PEN.

OH, AND I TOOK THE LIBERTY OF CHECKING OFF YOUR ETHNIC BACKGROUND AS ESKIMO. IT'S JUST A STATISTICAL THING.

1. DOES YOUR BOSS CLEARLY COMMUNICATE YOUR OBJECTIVES?

7-5

187

THAT'S OUR NEW "STRATEGIC DIVERSIFICATION FUND."

OUR LAWYERS PUT YOUR MONEY IN LITTLE BAGS, THEN WE HAVE TRAINED DOGS BURY THEM AROUND TOWN.

DO THEY BURY THE BAGS OR THE LAWYERS?

WE'VE TRIED IT BOTH WAYS.

I INVESTED ALL OF MY MONEY IN STOCK OPTIONS.

WHAT'S AN OPTION?

IT'S COMPLICATED... BASICALLY, YOU GIVE YOUR MONEY TO A STOCK BROKER AND HE BUYS NICE THINGS FOR HIS FAMILY.

DO YOU HAVE ANY SNIDE COMMENTS?

NO, YOU TOOK ALL THE FUN OUT OF IT.

AM I WRONG OR DID YOU TELL ME YOU INVESTED ALL OF YOUR MONEY IN STOCK OPTIONS FOR A COMPANY CALLED ZYMED?

YES.

THE RADIO SAYS THE STOCK PRICE TRIPLED ON TAKEOVER RUMORS. YOU JUST MADE ABOUT TEN MILLION DOLLARS.

BUT THEY SAY MONEY CAN'T BUY HAPPINESS.

APPARENTLY "THEY" ARE IDIOTS.

189

I'M GOING TO WORK LIKE A REGULAR GUY EVEN THOUGH I JUST MADE A FORTUNE IN THE STOCK MARKET.

THAT'S BECAUSE I STILL WANT TO BE A USEFUL AND CONTRIBUTING MEMBER OF SOCIETY.

7-13

AND OF COURSE, THE WORKPLACE IS THE SECOND MOST SATISFYING PLACE TO GLOAT.

ARE YOU DONE HERE YET?

© 1992 United Feature Syndicate, Inc.

I CAN'T HELP THINKING THAT MY NEW WEALTH WILL LEAD TO TRAGEDY.

© 1992 United Feature Syndicate, Inc.

IT SEEMS LIKE RICH PEOPLE ALWAYS HAVE HORRIBLE TRAGEDIES.

LIKE WHAT?

7-14

FLASH!

...LIKE BEING STRUCK BY LIGHTNING ON A CLEAR DAY.

INCOMING METEOR!!

I'VE HAD NOTHING BUT TRAGEDY SINCE MAKING A FORTUNE IN THE STOCK MARKET.

7-15

SOMETIMES, DOGBERT, IT SEEMS LIKE OUR LIVES HAVE PRESET BALANCES OF JOY AND PAIN; WHEN ONE GETS TOO HIGH THE OTHER KICKS IN TO COMPENSATE.

© 1992 United Feature Syndicate, Inc.

BUT THROUGH IT ALL, I ALWAYS HAVE YOU, MY FRIEND.

AT LEAST UNTIL MY GOOD LUCK KICKS IN.

GEE, MARY, YOU WEREN'T WILLING TO DATE ME BEFORE I MADE MILLIONS IN THE STOCK MARKET.

I'M AFRAID YOU SEE ME AS JUST A BIG, TALKING WALLET.

YOU'RE MUCH MORE THAN THAT.

FOR EXAMPLE, YOU ALSO WEAR THICK GLASSES.

TOO LITTLE, TOO LATE.

I'VE BEEN MISERABLE SINCE I MADE MY FORTUNE IN THE STOCK MARKET...

IT'S THE "LAW OF FOUND MONEY." NATURE WON'T ALLOW US TO KEEP MONEY WE FIND ON THE GROUND OR WIN BY CHANCE. DON'T RESIST; LET YOUR INTUITION GUIDE YOU.

THIS COMES WITH A COLOR MONITOR, RIGHT?

GRAY 9

ONLY $10,000,000

I SPENT MY ENTIRE FORTUNE TO BUY THIS SUPERCOMPUTER.

WHAT DOES IT DO?

IT CAN CALCULATE THE VALUE OF PI TO ABOUT A JILLION DECIMAL PLACES...

A LOT OF PEOPLE TALK ABOUT THE AREAS OF CIRCLES, BUT I'M DOING SOMETHING ABOUT IT.

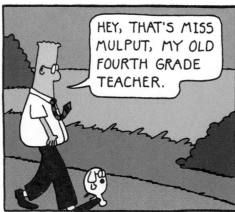

I'M USING MY NEW SUPERCOMPUTER TO CREATE A MODEL THAT CAN PREDICT YOUR ENTIRE LIFE.

YOU SEE, EVERYTHING, INCLUDING YOUR BRAIN CHEMISTRY, IS SUBJECT TO PREDICTABLE PATTERNS OF CAUSE AND EFFECT...

THAT'S RIDICULOUS. IT IMPLIES THAT WE HAVE NO FREE WILL.

NEXT, YOU START GETTING REALLY MAD AT ME.

7-20

HERE'S THE FULL SCRIPT OF THE REST OF YOUR LIFE. MY SUPERCOMPUTER MODEL PREDICTED IT.

7-21

WELL, ACCORDING TO THIS I'LL BE KIDNAPPED BY EVIL SQUIRRELS AND FORCED TO WORK IN THEIR NUT MINES.

THEY GET ME TOO.

I DIDN'T KNOW THAT EVIL SQUIRRELS HAD NUT MINES.

IT'S PROBABLY TOO LATE TO DO ANYTHING ABOUT IT.

THIS MAN USED HIS SUPERCOMPUTER TO PREDICT THE FUTURE OF THE WORLD.

WITHIN FIVE YEARS, EVIL SQUIRRELS WILL CONQUER THE WORLD AND MAKE US ALL SLAVES IN THEIR NUT MINES.

7-22

THE SQUIRRELS SHOULD LOVE THIS GUY.

IT'S BASED ON ACTUAL MATH.

PRAIRIE DOGS

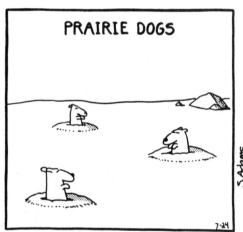

OFFICE WORKERS

PRAIRIE DOG WORKERS

DILBERT

By Scott Adams

NOW SHOWING
HANDS-OF-DEATH

Boycot

Boycot

WHY ARE YOU PROTESTING AGAINST THIS MOVIE?

Boycot

IT PORTRAYS RED HEADS AS HOT TEMPERED AND IGNORANT.

Boycot

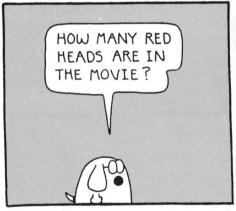

HOW MANY RED HEADS ARE IN THE MOVIE?

ONE. BUT THE POINT IS, RED HEADS DON'T FIT THEIR STEREOTYPE OF BEING HOT TEMPERED AND IGNORANT.

Boycot

ACTUALLY, IGNORANCE WAS NEVER A STEREOTYPE OF RED HEADS UNTIL YOU BROUGHT IT UP HERE.

7-26

SEAN, YOU IDIOT! I TOLD YOU!

SHUT UP, DENNIS! I'LL POUND YOU TO A PULP!!

Boycot

Boycot

AND "BOYCOTT" IS SPELLED WITH A DOUBLE "T."

WHAT'S THIS?

I'M STARTING MY OWN NEWSLETTER FOR CLUELESS PEOPLE.

THANKS TO THE TECHNICAL MARVEL OF DESKTOP PUBLISHING, CLUELESS PEOPLE WILL NOW HAVE THE BENEFIT OF MY IMMENSE WISDOM.

HOW DO YOU KNOW WHO THE CLUELESS PEOPLE ARE?

THEY ASK A LOT OF QUESTIONS.

BOB, HERE'S A COPY OF MY NEW NEWSLETTER FOR CLUELESS PEOPLE.

"DOGBERT'S CLUES FOR THE CLUELESS:
1. PROFESSIONAL WRESTLING IS ALL FAKED.
2. NOBODY EVER LOST WEIGHT ON A HOME EXERCISE DEVICE."

"3. LOOKS ARE MORE IMPORTANT TO HAPPINESS THAN BRAINS
4. IF PEOPLE DON'T COMMENT ON YOUR NEW HAIRDO, THEY HATE IT."

IT'S NOT HEALTHY TO READ THEM ALL AT ONCE, BOB.

WELL, THERE YOU ARE, WORKING ON YOUR LITTLE NEWSLETTER FOR CLUELESS PEOPLE...

YOU'RE PROBABLY THINKING UP SOME CLEVER LITTLE FACT THAT THE SO-CALLED CLUELESS PEOPLE WOULD NEVER REALIZE ON THEIR OWN.

LET ME SEE... "IF YOU ARE THE ONLY ONE TALKING THEN IT IS A CLUE THAT NO CONVERSATION IS OCCURRING AND IT IS TIME TO LEAVE."

RATBERT, I BROUGHT YOU A COPY OF THE "DOGBERT CLUELETTER," THE NEWSLETTER FOR CLUELESS PEOPLE.

NO THANKS. I USED TO BE CLUELESS BUT I TURNED THAT SITUATION AROUND 360 DEGREES.

"DOGBERT'S CLUES TO CONVERSATIONAL GEOMETRY..."

ALICE, MARY, LET'S GO TO THE LADIES ROOM!

I RENTED "GONE WITH THE WIND." WE CAN WATCH IT ON THE BIG SCREEN TV

I WANT THE GREY SOFA!

HEY, LOOK! THE MEN'S ROOM HAS SOAP!!

I THOUGHT I WAS HAPPY...

THEN I THOUGHT WHAT IF I ONLY THINK I'M HAPPY BUT I'M NOT. MAYBE I'VE BEEN HYPNOTIZED AND DON'T EVEN KNOW IT.

WORRYING ABOUT IT MADE ME UNHAPPY, WHICH MEANS I MUST NOT BE UNDER HYPNOSIS, SO I'M HAPPY.

MAYBE I ONLY THINK YOU'RE TALKING BUT REALLY I'M HAPPY.

DILBERT

By Scott Adams

NATURE IS SO WONDERFUL...

THEY SAY WE DON'T LEAVE THE PLANET TO FUTURE GENERATIONS, WE BORROW IT FROM OUR CHILDREN.

IT'S EVEN BETTER THAN THAT.

WE DON'T HAVE CHILDREN, SO WE'RE BORROWING THE PLANET FROM COMPLETE STRANGERS!

AND THERE'S NO COLLATERAL. WE CAN USE UP THE PLANET, HAVE GREAT LIVES AND LEAVE AN EMPTY SMOKING SHELL TO THE STRANGERS!

I TELL YOU, PEOPLE HAVE COMPLETELY OVERLOOKED THE POSITIVE SIDE OF THIS ENVIRONMENT SITUATION.

BUT SOMEDAY I WANT TO HAVE CHILDREN.

LET'S HOPE THEY'RE NOT AS SELFISH AS YOU.

GEE, TIM, YOU LOOK AWFUL.

I'VE BEEN WORKING FOR FIVE DAYS WITHOUT ANY SLEEP TO FINISH THIS REPORT.

AT FIRST I HAD A MENTAL BLOCK. BUT ON THE FOURTH DAY I WAS VISITED BY AN INCAN MONKEY GOD WHO TOLD ME WHAT TO WRITE.

WOW, LUCKY BREAK.

NOW I JUST HAVE TO FIND SOMEBODY WHO CAN TRANSLATE HIS SIMPLE BUT BEAUTIFUL LANGUAGE.

I UNDERSTAND YOU'VE BEEN GOING WITHOUT SLEEP OR FOOD FOR DAYS JUST TO MEET SOME ARTIFICIAL DEADLINE.

ERGLE, FLUMG

AS A RESULT, YOUR WORK HAS BEEN MUDDLE-BRAINED AND INCOMPREHENSIBLE. YOU LEAVE ME NO CHOICE, TIM.

GLEEB, NUB

TIM GOT PROMOTED TO DIVISION MANAGER.

I WONDER IF HE KNOWS IT.

I'VE SACRIFICED MY HEALTH, MY PERSONAL LIFE AND MY SOUL TO GET PROMOTED.

HA HA HA! BUT IT WAS ALL WORTH IT BECAUSE I HAVE AN OFFICE WITH A <u>DOOR</u> AND YOU STILL WORK IN A CUBICLE!

MAYBE I'LL HOST A SPECIAL "LOW-ACHIEVER DAY" TO LET YOU TOUCH MY DOOR.

OOPS

A FARMER IN WINDHAM CLAIMS THAT THE FACE OF SAINT THERESA APPEARED IN A CAN OF VARNISH.

WORSHIPERS ARE FLOCKING TO THE FARM TO WITNESS THE MIRACLE. "I SHOULD CHARGE FOR ADMISSION" QUIPPED THE FARMER.

GUESS WHAT I FOUND IN THE PEANUT BUTTER.

PLEASE, LET IT BE A BUG

IT'S A MIRACLE, RATBERT. THE IMAGE OF SAINT TED APPEARED IN MY JAR OF PEANUT BUTTER!

SAINT TED? WHO EVER HEARD OF SAINT TED? COULDN'T YOU GET SAINT THERESA?

SHE WAS BOOKED TO A CAN OF VARNISH IN UPSTATE NEW YORK.

SAINT TED LOOKS LIKE A "HAPPY FACE."

PEOPLE HAVE TRAVELED FROM ALL OVER TO SEE THE MIRACLE OF THE PEANUT BUTTER.

STEP RIGHT UP... JUST TEN BUCKS TO SEE THE FACE OF SAINT TED APPEARING IN MY JAR OF PEANUT BUTTER.

$10

OOH! AND I SEE ELVIS IN THE JELLO!

ONLY THE KING MOVES LIKE THAT!

DILBERT

By Scott Adams

WHY SHOULD I HIRE YOU AS MY CONSULTANT?

I'LL USE MY SPECIAL PROCESS OF COGNITIVE DISSONANCE TO IMPROVE EMPLOYEE MORALE.

HOW DOES IT WORK?

WHEN PEOPLE ARE IN AN ABSURD SITUATION, THEIR MINDS RATIONALIZE IT BY INVENTING A COMFORTABLE ILLUSION.

OKAY, GO DO IT.

ISN'T IT STRANGE THAT YOU HAVE THIS DEAD END JOB WHEN YOU'RE TWICE AS SMART AS YOUR BOSS?

THE HOURS ARE LONG, THE PAY IS MEDIOCRE, NOBODY RESPECTS YOUR CONTRIBUTIONS, AND YET YOU FREELY CHOOSE TO WORK HERE.

IT'S ABSURD! NO, WAIT... THERE MUST BE A REASON... I MUST WORK HERE BECAUSE I LOVE THE WORK.

I LOVE THIS JOB.

NEXT!

THE MIGHTY WARRIOR PREPARES FOR BATTLE...

TODAY, BOLD MEMOS WILL BE WRITTEN, DANGEROUS MEETINGS WILL BE ATTENDED, AND MANY A PHOTOCOPIED IMAGE WILL BE CAPTURED FOR ETERNITY.

IF IT WEREN'T FOR SARCASM, MY LIFE WOULD SOUND PATHETIC.

GLAD TO HELP.

I HAVEN'T DATED MUCH SINCE I CAME DOWN WITH PUPPETITIS.

IT'S A RARE DISORDER THAT MAKES YOUR HAND ACT LIKE A PUPPET.

THAT'S WEIRD.

HE HATES US! WE MUST KILL HIM!

NOT YET, GINGER!

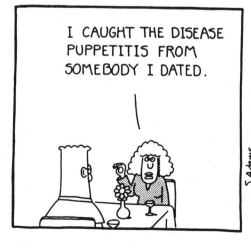

I CAUGHT THE DISEASE PUPPETITIS FROM SOMEBODY I DATED.

HA HA! THAT'S RIGHT! NOW HER HAND IS A PUPPET!

I HATE THE NINETIES.

JOIN US... DON'T BE AFRAID.

DILBERT

By Scott Adams

DILBERT, I'D LIKE YOU TO MEET BEN, OUR NEWEST FAST-TRACK MANAGER.

HI

BEN HAS NO REAL EXPERIENCE BUT HE'S VERY TALL, SO WE KNOW HE'LL GO FAR.

I ALSO HAVE EXECUTIVE STYLE HAIR.

WE THINK IT WILL TURN SILVER.

HEY, I HAVEN'T DONE A THING FOR MINUTES AND YET I STILL GET PAID.

HOO-HOO-HA! I'M RIPPING OFF THE EVIL CORPORATE EMPIRE AND THERE'S NOTHING THEY CAN DO ABOUT IT! I HAVE TOTAL POWER!

I'D BETTER KEEP THIS LITTLE SECRET TO MYSELF.

HEY, I'M GETTING PAID FOR DOING NOTHING!

HERE'S SOMETHING ELSE THAT'S TOTALLY UNIMPORTANT YET REQUIRES ACTION.

I'LL ROUTE IT TO A SUBORDINATE, THUS INFLATING ITS PERCEIVED IMPORTANCE AND DESTROYING BOTH MORALE AND PRODUCTIVITY.

WHAT LUCK, I GOT TWO COPIES!

DILBERT

By Scott Adams

THE PROBLEM WITH MODERN SOCIETY IS THAT WE HAVE NO TRADITIONS.

WE SHOULD CREATE SOME TRADITIONS FOR FUTURE GENER-ATIONS.

HOW DO YOU CREATE A TRADITION?

WELL, YOU JUST DO SOMETHING RIDICULOUS EVERY YEAR AT THE SAME TIME.

EVENTUALLY OTHER PEOPLE JOIN IN AND THEN IT'S A TRADITION.

OOH, HOW ABOUT "ANNUAL NOSE-SAUSAGE DAY"? YOU DRESS IN COLORFUL ROBES AND STICK SAUSAGES IN YOUR NOSE!

8-30

YES, YES... AND WE'LL DO A SQUIRREL DANCE AND SHOUT "KALOO-KALAH" AT THE SUN!

© 1992 United Feature Syndicate, Inc.

OR MAYBE NOT.

YOU LOST ME WITH THE SQUIRREL DANCE.

I'M SENDING ALL OF YOU TO THE "RIVERS AND TREES" MANAGEMENT COURSE.

THERE YOU'LL BE ASKED TO PERFORM A VARIETY OF DANGEROUS TASKS IN THE WOODS. YOUR SURVIVAL WILL DEPEND ON YOUR CREATIVITY AND ABILITY TO WORK TOGETHER.

8-31

OH, SO IT'S A TEAM-BUILDING EXERCISE.

I THINK OF IT MORE AS A HEADCOUNT REDUCTION THING.

AT THE "RIVERS AND TREES" MANAGEMENT COURSE.

WE'LL START WITH A TRUST-BUILDING EXERCISE.

YOU HAVE ONE MINUTE TO DECIDE TO EAT THESE DONUTS OR TO SAVE YOUR CO-WORKER FROM THE BEAR.

OKAY, WHO WANTS TO BE ON THE DONUT OPTION WORKING COMMITTEE?

OOPS... PROBLEM SOLVED.

9-1

AT THE "RIVERS AND TREES" MANAGEMENT COURSE.

NEXT, WE HAVE A CREATIVITY EXERCISE.

YOUR TASK IS TO BUILD A COMMERCIAL AIRPORT LANDING STRIP USING NOTHING BUT A LEAF AND A DEAD BEE.

9-2

LOOK, WE ALREADY VOTED. WE'RE DESIGN AND YOU'RE CONSTRUCTION.

TIME.

AT THE "RIVERS AND TREES" MANAGEMENT COURSE.

THIS NEXT EXERCISE IS ALWAYS A FAVORITE.

USING ONLY A ROPE, YOUR TEAM MUST FIGURE OUT HOW TO CROSS THE MUDDY PATCH WITHOUT GETTING YOUR FEET DIRTY.

I COULD HAVE BEEN A FOREST RANGER, BUT NO-O-O-O...

I'M CHANNELING ALL OF MY PAIN AND HOSTILITY INTO MY ART.

ALL I SEE IS A BOWL OF FRUIT.

THE BANANA HATES THE APPLE.

TELL ME WHAT YOU THINK, AND DON'T TRY TO SPARE MY FEELINGS.

It's a hideous compost of random colors. It seems both hackneyed and poorly executed. It's an embarrassing proof of your utter lack of talent.

AS FOR YOU PERSONALLY, SPEND SOME TIME ON A "STAIRMASTER."

STICK TO THE ART, PLEASE!

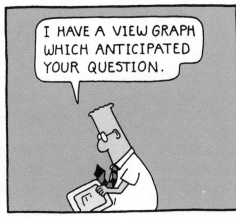

IT'S CALLED MULTIMEDIA, DOGBERT. NOW I CAN INCLUDE VIDEO AND MUSIC WITH MY COMPUTER PROGRAMS.

THIS MORNING I ADDED MY FACE PLUS THE THEME SONG FROM "STAR WARS" TO MY BUDGET SPREAD-SHEET.

I ALREADY FORGOT HOW I SURVIVED WITHOUT IT.

IT CAN GET PRETTY UGLY WHEN SCIENCE AND ART COLLIDE.

WHEN I STARTED PROGRAMMING, WE DIDN'T HAVE ANY OF THESE SISSY "ICONS" AND "WINDOWS."

ALL WE HAD WERE ZEROS AND ONES -- AND SOMETIMES WE DIDN'T EVEN HAVE ONES.

I WROTE AN ENTIRE DATABASE PROGRAM USING ONLY ZEROS.

YOU HAD ZEROS? WE HAD TO USE THE LETTER "O."

I'M TESTING MY THEORY THAT GOOD ADVERTISING CAN SELL ANYTHING.

SO I ASKED MYSELF "WHAT IS THE THING LEAST DESIRED ON EARTH?"

LADIES! DATE A DILBERT CALL 510-803-9338

QUANTITIES ARE LIMITED

HMM...

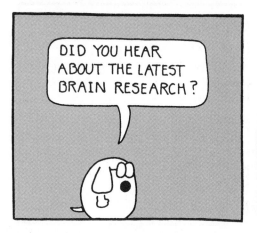

WE MUST USE ALL OF THE RESOURCES OF THE "COW AND EGG" LOBBY TO COUNTER THE LATEST THREAT FROM THE VEGETARIANS.

SOMEHOW THEY'VE MANAGED TO LINK FOOD WITH HEALTH... THEY INVENTED A "NUTRITION PYRAMID" CHART AND GOT SCHOOLS TO USE IT...

9-14

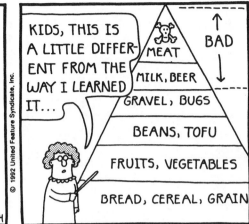

KIDS, THIS IS A LITTLE DIFFERENT FROM THE WAY I LEARNED IT...

BAD

MEAT
MILK, BEER
GRAVEL, BUGS
BEANS, TOFU
FRUITS, VEGETABLES
BREAD, CEREAL, GRAIN

© 1992 United Feature Syndicate, Inc.

DOGBERT, WE NEED YOU TO BECOME THE CHARISMATIC LEADER OF OUR VEGETARIAN MOVEMENT.

9-15

WE TRIED TO PICK A LEADER FROM OUR RANKS, BUT MOST OF US ARE ... UH... WELL...

© 1992 United Feature Syndicate, Inc.

SCRAWNY WIMPS?

YEAH, BUT DECEPTIVELY HEALTHY.

DOGBERT, I DON'T UNDERSTAND WHY YOU, OR ANYBODY, WOULD BECOME A VEGETARIAN.

9-16

YOU MEAN, WHY DON'T I TAKE DEAD ANIMALS, COOK THEM UNTIL THEY BECOME CARCINOGENIC, THEN EAT THEM INSTEAD OF SOMETHING NUTRITIOUS? IS THAT YOUR QUESTION?

© 1992 United Feature Syndicate, Inc.

EXACTLY. IS THERE ANY GOOD REASON? HAVE YOU JOINED A CULT?

APPARENTLY.

DILBERT

By Scott Adams

HA HA! NOW SPIN ON YOUR HEAD! HA HA HA!

WHAT'S GOING ON HERE?

THIS IS YERGI. HE'S VISITING FROM ELBONIA.

THE ECONOMY IN ELBONIA IS SO BAD HE ONLY EARNS THREE DOLLARS A MONTH AS A DOCTOR.

IT TAKES A YEAR TO EARN ENOUGH FOR A PAIR OF SHOES... IT TAKES TWO YEARS FOR A POUND OF MEAT.

PHILANTHROPIST THAT I AM, I OFFERED TO GIVE HIM AN OLD BOOT IF HE WOULD ACT LIKE MY TRAINED MONKEY FOR A WEEK.

DOGBERT! I CAN'T BELIEVE YOU WOULD BUY THIS MAN'S DIGNITY FOR AN OLD BOOT!

9-20

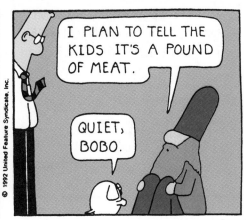

I PLAN TO TELL THE KIDS IT'S A POUND OF MEAT.

QUIET, BOBO.

S. Adams

219

THERE... I THINK I'VE INVENTED A WAY TO SEND VAST AMOUNTS OF DATA WITHOUT FIBER OPTIC CABLES.

IT'S A SIMPLE APPLICATION OF J.S. BELL'S THEOREM.* HE SHOWED THAT IF YOU BREAK UP A MOLECULE AND CHANGE THE SPIN OF ONE ELECTRON, THE SPIN OF THE OTHER ELECTRONS ORIGINALLY JOINED WILL IMMEDIATELY CHANGE TOO, NO MATTER WHERE THEY ARE.

*Really, no kidding.

WHAT DO YOU THINK THE FIBER OPTIC INDUSTRY WILL GIVE ME FOR THIS?

A HORSE'S HEAD IN YOUR BED.

FROM THE LOOKS OF YOUR GARBAGE, YOU'VE INVENTED SOME SORT OF MOLECULE BIFURCATION COMMUNICATOR.

AH, YES, EINSTEIN THOUGHT THIS TYPE OF THING MIGHT WORK. PHYSICIST JOHN STUART BELL KIND OF FLESHED IT OUT IN 1964. BUT YOU'VE REALLY ADDED SOMETHING...

SPECIFICALLY, YOU'VE ADDED THIS CALCULATION ERROR HERE.

HIS NAME IS DILBERT. HE INVENTED SOMETHING THAT WOULD MAKE OUR ENTIRE PRODUCT LINE OBSOLETE.

DO YOU HAVE A PLAN?

UH... I COULD WAX YOUR DESK WITH MY HAIR AGAIN.

IT'S JUST CRAZY ENOUGH TO WORK.

220

I'VE RECEIVED DEATH THREATS BECAUSE OF MY NEW PATENT. SO I AUGMENTED OUR HOME SECURITY SYSTEM.

THE SIDEWALK IS RIGGED TO GIVE AN ELECTRIC SHOCK, THUS DISARMING THE INTRUDER. THEN A SPRING CATAPULTS HIM TO THE CITY LANDFILL.

AAGH! FLING!

THE MAIL IS HERE.

I HEARD YOU'RE LOOKING FOR A HIT MAN TO ELIMINATE AN INVENTOR NAMED DILBERT.

FOR A MILLION DOLLARS I CAN DELIVER HIS HEAD ON A PLATTER.

DOES IT HAVE TO BE ON A PLATTER?

I'VE TRIED USING THOSE TUPPERWARE LETTUCE CRISPERS, BUT IT LOSES A LOT OF THE DRAMA.

HERE IS PHOTO PROOF THAT I COMPLETED MY HIT-MAN CONTRACT ON DILBERT.

EXCELLENT.

HERE HE IS, SITTING LIFELESS IN HIS STUFFED CHAIR.

IT LOOKS LIKE HE'S JUST WATCHING TELEVISION.

TECHNICALLY, MY CONTRACT DOESN'T SAY I MUST KILL HIM. IT SAYS I MUST "PROVE HE HAS NO LIFE."

DILBERT
By Scott Adams

DETECTIVE RESEARCH ON YOUR POTENTIAL ROMANTIC PARTNER

I'M CONSIDERING DATING A MAN, BUT I'M WORRIED.

WHAT'S HIS NAME?

BILL... HIS NAME IS BILL.

AHH... BILL... YES, I KNOW ALL ABOUT BILL.

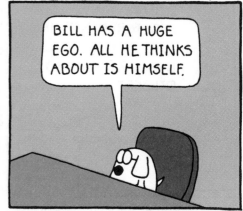

BILL HAS A HUGE EGO. ALL HE THINKS ABOUT IS HIMSELF.

HE HAS NO EMOTIONAL DEPTH AND HE THINKS OF YOUR CONVERSATIONS AS MERE CHATTER. HE WANTS YOUR BODY, NOT YOUR MIND.

SEVERAL TIMES A DAY, BILL IMAGINES HIMSELF WITH DIFFERENT WOMEN.

DARN. THIS TIME I THOUGHT I'D FOUND A NORMAL GUY.

I HAVE SOME REALLY BAD NEWS FOR YOU.

I'VE DECIDED TO BECOME A DEMAGOGUE.

I'LL FIND SOME ISSUE THAT APPEALS TO THE EMOTIONS AND BLIND PREJUDICES OF THE MASSES, THEN I'LL WHIP IT INTO A MEDIA FRENZY AND BECOME A NATIONAL FIGURE.

FOR EXAMPLE, UNMARRIED MEN ARE RESPONSIBLE FOR MOST OF OF OUR VIOLENT CRIMES.

THAT'S BECAUSE WE TEND TO HAVE PETS.

9-28

"UNMARRIED MEN COMMIT NINETY PERCENT OF ALL VIOLENT ACTS. THEY SHOULD ALL BE JAILED IN ADVANCE TO PREVENT FURTHER ATROCITIES."

"AND I SHOULD BECOME A MEDIA SENSATION FOR SUGGESTING SUCH A PROVOCATIVE THING.

THE END "

IT'S HARD TO WRITE A WHOLE BOOK WHEN YOU'RE AS GIFTED AS I AM AT GETTING TO THE POINT.

9-29

MY GUEST FOR TODAY'S SHOW IS DOGBERT, AUTHOR OF THE ONE-PAGE BOOK "UNMARRIED MEN ARE SCUM."

YOUR THEORY IS THAT ALL UNMARRIED MEN SHOULD BE JAILED FOR LIFE, THUS ENDING MOST CRIME.

EXACTLY.

WHAT IF THEY TRY TO BEAT THE SYSTEM BY GETTING MARRIED?

SERVES 'EM RIGHT.

9-30

I'M FOLLOWING IN YOUR FOOTSTEPS SO I CAN BE A DEMAGOGUE TOO.

YOUR BOOK "UNMARRIED MEN ARE SCUM" WAS SO SUCCESSFUL THAT I DECIDED TO WRITE MY OWN HATE BOOK DISGUISED AS SCIENCE!

10-1

I CALL IT "MOLES ARE MORONS."

WERE YOU AWARE THAT MOLES HAVE A STRONG UNDERGROUND MOVEMENT?

I MUST WARN YOU THAT I HAVE AN OBSESSIVE PERSONALITY.

IF I SPEND A MOMENT WITH A MAN I FALL COMPLETELY IN LOVE. I THINK OF ONLY HIM. I... I BECOME HIS SLAVE.

10-2

ARE YOU SAYING...

YES. I'M IN LOVE WITH OUR WAITER.

HAVE YOU EVER HAD A STRANGE DREAM OR A NOSEBLEED?

YES.

IT'S CLEAR THAT YOU'RE SUPPRESSING MEMORIES OF BEING ABDUCTED BY ALIENS. I CAN USE HYPNOSIS TO GET AT THOSE MEMORIES.

10-3

WHAT IF THE HYPNOSIS ITSELF MAKES ME THINK IT HAPPENED WHEN IT DIDN'T? I'LL BE SCORNED AND RIDICULED FOR LIFE.

THAT'S A RISK I'M WILLING TO TAKE.

DILBERT

By Scott Adams

Do you think it's better to be smart or good-looking, Dogbert.

I've been both for so long, it's hard to be objective.

It's hypothetical. Suppose you had to pick one.

I'd stay as I am: smart, good-looking and talented.

You can't add stuff. You have to start with nothing and pick either brains or good looks.

And witty too... smart, good-looking, talented and witty.

No, no, no... suppose you had NONE of those qualities. What would you do then?

I'd probably annoy my dog. Same as you.

S. Adams

10-4

© 1992 United Feature Syndicate, Inc.

YOU ARE IN A DEEP SLEEP... NOW, WHILE UNDER HYPNOSIS YOU CAN DRAW THE ALIENS WHO ABDUCTED YOU.

HINT: THEY ALL LOOK EXACTLY LIKE "E.T."

10-5

WOW! I DREW THAT??

THEY USUALLY COME BACK FOR YOU. BETTER KEEP A BAG PACKED.

I DIDN'T REMEMBER BEING ABDUCTED BY ALIENS UNTIL YOU HYPNOTIZED ME. BUT NOW I REMEMBER THEY LOOKED LIKE "E.T."

I REMEMBER BEING IN A DARK ROOM WITH ROWS OF SEATS. THEY FED US A POPCORN-LIKE SUBSTANCE. MY FEET WERE STUCK TO THE FLOOR.

10-6

I RECALL BEING DISGUSTED THAT THEY CHARGED ME SIX DOLLARS TO ENTER THE SHIP.

THAT'S WHY YOU SUPPRESSED THE MEMORY.

I'M A GENERAL FROM THE DEPARTMENT OF GOVERNMENT COVER-UPS.

IF YOU TELL YOUR U.F.O. ABDUCTION STORY TO THE PRESS WE'LL SLAY YOU WITH UNTRACEABLE POISON.

10-7

I DON'T THINK I'M GETTING A GOOD VALUE FOR MY TAX DOLLAR HERE.

BREATH MINT?

THE GOVERNMENT SENT A GENERAL TO KILL ME FOR TALKING ABOUT MY ENCOUNTER WITH SPACE ALIENS.

I WAS SCARED AT FIRST. BUT WHEN YOU THINK ABOUT THE GOVERNMENT'S TRACK RECORD, WELL, MY ODDS ARE PRETTY GOOD...

10-8

ESPECIALLY AFTER ALL THE BUDGET CUTBACKS.

DANG IT! WHERE'S MY AIR SUPPORT?!!

GENERAL, I DON'T UNDERSTAND WHY THE GOVERNMENT IS TRYING TO COVER UP ALL THE U.F.O. ENCOUNTERS.

PEOPLE WOULD LOSE FAITH IN THEIR GOVERNMENT IF THEY KNEW ALIENS WERE ABDUCTING PEOPLE AND WE WERE HELPLESS TO STOP THEM.

10-9

SO, TO MAINTAIN CONFIDENCE IN THE GOVERNMENT, YOU USE OUR TAXES TO KILL THE CITIZENS WHO FIND OUT?

IS THAT SO BAD?

WE CAN ONLY SPECULATE WHY ALIENS KEEP ABDUCTING PEOPLE.

THEY OFTEN PROBE PEOPLE'S BODY CAVITIES. SOMETIMES THEY IMPLANT SMALL OBJECTS. IT MUST BE SOME FORM OF HIGHLY ADVANCED MEDICAL RESEARCH.

10-10

HOW ABOUT ANOTHER ROUND OF "HIDE THE PELLET"?

OKAY. I CAN USE MY NOSE PROBER.

DILBERT

By Scott Adams

PARENT LICENSES

WE'D BETTER CHECK IT OUT.

WHY DO WE NEED A LICENSE TO BECOME PARENTS?

SOMETHING HAD TO BE DONE.

UNDER THE OLD SYSTEM ALL YOU NEEDED TO BE A PARENT WAS A FEW BODY PARTS AND A BRAIN THE SIZE OF A GARBANZO BEAN.

SO I DEVELOPED THIS WRITTEN TEST TO WEED OUT THE MAJOR BOZOS.

IF A BABY CRIES, YOU SHOULD:
A. FEED IT
B. DISCIPLINE IT
C. CALL IT "STUPID"

YOU HAVE TO SHOW IT WHO'S THE BOSS.

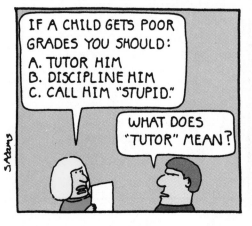

IF A CHILD GETS POOR GRADES YOU SHOULD:
A. TUTOR HIM
B. DISCIPLINE HIM
C. CALL HIM "STUPID."

WHAT DOES "TUTOR" MEAN?

S. Adams

AN ACCEPTABLE NICKNAME FOR A CHILD IS:
A. JUNIOR
B. UGLY
C. STUPID

DEPENDS IF IT'S A BOY.

10-11

WELL? CAN WE BE PARENTS?

NO. AND YOU'LL HAVE TO LEAVE SOME BODY PARTS AT THE FRONT DESK.

SOMEWHERE OUT THERE IS THE WOMAN WHO IS PERFECT FOR ME.

BUT HOW WILL I RECOGNIZE HER? HOW WILL I KNOW SHE'S THE ONE?

MEANWHILE, SOMEWHERE "OUT THERE"...

OKAY, I AGREE THAT IT SEEMS LIKE CATS OWN PEOPLE, BUT IT'S NOT ACTUALLY THE LAW.

THEY SAY EVERYBODY HAS A PERFECT ROMANTIC MATCH...

AND THEY SAY THE KEY TO A LIFE OF HAPPINESS...

...IS TO AVOID THAT PERSON AT ALL COSTS.

YUCK   YUCK   YUCK   YUCK

UH-OH... I SMELL A CREATIVE IDEA BEING FORMED SOMEWHERE IN THE BUILDING.

SNIFF SNIFF

I MUST FIND IT AND CRUSH IT.

HEY, THIS IS NEW.

IT'S A TRAP!!

SUGGESTION BOX

I JUST RECEIVED YOUR EMPLOYEE SUGGESTION.

WE'LL HANDLE IT THE USUAL WAY -- BY MAKING YOU SIT UNDER A WET BLANKET SURROUNDED BY IMBECILES.

10-15

AT LEAST THERE'S A PROCESS.

EXPLAIN YOUR SUGGESTION AGAIN.

© 1992 United Feature Syndicate, Inc.

MOST HANDSOME MEN ARE SELF-CENTERED JERKS.

BUT YOU'RE DIFFERENT... YOU'RE ...

10-16

CONSIDERATE?

UGLY.

© 1992 United Feature Syndicate, Inc.

REMEMBER THE TIME YOU LAUGHED AT YOUR OWN JOKE SO HARD THAT YOU INHALED AND SNORTED AT THE SAME TIME?

NEWS

© 1992 United Feature Syndicate, Inc.

THEN YOU CHOKED ON YOUR OWN SPIT, WHICH CAUSED YOU TO LURCH OVER AND BONK YOUR HEAD ON THE COFFEE TABLE...

I'M IGNORING YOU.

WHO SAYS YOUR LIFE IS BORING?

NEWS

10-17

I'M COLLECTING MONEY FOR MARY'S BIRTHDAY GIFT.

HOW MUCH DO YOU WANT?

OH, IT'S TOTALLY UP TO YOU.

HOWEVER, THE USUAL ACCEPTED LEVELS ARE, IN EFFECT...

TEN DOLLARS FROM HER BOSS AND ANYBODY ELSE WHO THINKS IT WOULD IMPROVE HIS ODDS OF BECOMING ROMANTICALLY INVOLVED WITH HER.

FIVE DOLLARS FROM MALE CO-WORKERS WHO FEEL THEIR MANHOOD WOULD BE THREATENED BY A SMALLER GIFT...

ONE DOLLAR IF YOU'RE A SECRETARY OR IF NOBODY IS WATCHING...

OR YOU CAN JUST RUFFLE THE MONEY ALREADY IN THE ENVELOPE AND ACT LIKE YOU GAVE FIVE.

10-18

LET'S SAY YOU FALL INTO MORE THAN ONE OF THOSE CATEGORIES...

ENGINEERS...

Ruffle Ruffle

I'VE DECIDED TO BECOME A DOCTOR.

PEOPLE HAVE TO SUCK UP TO DOCTORS, OTHERWISE THEY STICK BIG NEEDLES INTO YOUR BODY FOR PRACTICALLY NO REASON AT ALL.

A LOT OF CAREERS DON'T OFFER THAT KIND OPPORTUNITY.

YEAH, IT'S NOT THE SAME WITH A STAPLER.

10-19

HOLD STILL WHILE DOCTOR DOGBERT WHACKS YOUR KNEE.

10-20

AAK... CRIME IS SOCIETY'S FAULT... RAISE TAXES TO FEED THE POOR... STOP NUCLEAR RESEARCH... SAVE THE...

TAP

APPARENTLY YOU'RE A KNEE-JERK LIBERAL. YOU CAN LIVE A NORMAL LIFE BUT YOU'LL BE ANNOYING AT PARTIES.

YOU HAVE A MILD FLU, AND NORMALLY YOU WOULD SURVIVE.

HOWEVER, IN THIS BRIEF VISIT I'VE DEVELOPED NO REAL EMPATHY FOR YOU, SO I'VE DECIDED TO LET YOU DIE.

IS THERE ANYTHING I CAN DO?!

WELL... UNLESS YOU CAN AFFORD MY NEW "AMBASSADOR CLASS" SERVICE.

10-21

ATTENTION, ALL PATIENTS!

I HAVE TURBOCHARGED THE X-RAY MACHINE AND AIMED IT AT THE WAITING ROOM. EVERYBODY CLOSE YOUR EYES FOR FIVE MINUTES THEN LEAVE. YOUR DIAGNOSES WILL ARRIVE BY MAIL.

IT WAS A STROKE OF GENIUS TO SCHEDULE ALL OF THE HYPOCHON-DRIACS FOR THE SAME HOUR.

DOGBERT'S DATING SERVICE

I'D LIKE TO SIGN UP.

ALTHOUGH DEEP DOWN I KNOW THAT ALL OF THE PEOPLE IN YOUR SERVICE ARE MEN, I CLING TO THE FANTASY OF MEETING THE WOMAN WHO MODELED FOR YOUR BROCHURE.

SHE'S TAKEN, BUT I CAN MATCH YOU WITH SOMEBODY NAMED "FRANCIS" OR "KRIS."

THERE'S HOPE!

I'LL SEARCH MY DATE-A-BASE FOR WOMEN WHO WANT A NICE GUY AND DON'T CARE ABOUT LOOKS.

ALL I'M GETTING ARE SOME QUOTES FROM GUESTS ON "DONAHUE," BUT THEY DON'T SEEM SINCERE.

MAYBE IF I EXPAND THE SEARCH TO INCLUDE ALL PRIMATES...

WHY DID YOU ADD "DON'T CARE ABOUT LOOKS"?

DILBERT
By Scott Adams

DILBERT, I THINK IT WOULD BE BETTER IF WE WERE JUST FRIENDS.
OKAY.
OKAY?? HE TOOK IT TOO EASY. I SHOULD BARGAIN FOR MORE.
I MEAN... FRIENDS WITH OTHER PEOPLE. YOU AND I WOULD JUST BE ACQUAINT-ANCES.
OKAY.
STILL TOO EASY. I CAN GET MORE.
I DON'T MEAN THE KIND OF ACQUAINTANCES THAT COULD BECOME FRIENDS... IT WOULD BE MORE LIKE YOU WERE AN EX-EMPLOYEE OF MINE.
OKAY.
YEAH, THAT'S IT. YOU CAN BE MY EX-BUTLER, WHO I FIRED FOR STEALING STUFF.
S.Adams
OKAY.
10-25
© 1992 United Feature Syndicate, Inc.
WHAT'S GOING ON HERE?
GOOD. IT LOOKS LIKE THE WINDOW OF OPPORTUNITY IS STILL SLIGHTLY OPEN.

SO, YOU'RE A TIME MANAGEMENT EXPERT HUH? MIGHT BE USEFUL... I'LL LET YOU KNOW...

DECIDE NOW! DO IT! DO IT, DO IT! NOW NOW NOW NOW!

10-26

YOU'RE GOOD... WHEN CAN YOU START?

I'LL GET BACK TO YOU.

S. Adams

WELCOME TO THE "DOGBERT TIME MANAGEMENT LECTURE SERIES."

SORRY I'M AN HOUR LATE, BUT I WAS GIVING ANOTHER LECTURE ACROSS TOWN... IN EFFECT, I'LL COMPLETE TWO JOBS WHILE YOU SIT IN THE DARK LIKE STUNNED CATTLE.

I DON'T MEAN TO RUB IT IN, BUT MOOOO...

10-27

EVERY PERSON HAS NATURAL DAILY RHYTHMS OF MENTAL PEAKS AND TROUGHS. WE CAN USE THIS KNOWLEDGE TO IMPROVE YOUR PERFORMANCE.

10-28

WE USE HOURLY BODY TEMPERATURE READINGS TO IDENTIFY AND AVOID THE TROUGHS.

One O'clock. We have encountered a severe trough. I fear it could be the dreaded "El Niño" trough.

Panel 1: I'M AFRAID YOUR COMPANY IS BEING HIT BY AN EL NIÑO CIRCADIAN TROUGH.

WHAT'S THAT?

Panel 2: ONCE A DECADE, THE NATURAL BODY RHYTHMS OF ALL THE EMPLOYEES REACH THEIR MENTAL LOW POINT AT THE SAME TIME.

Panel 3: IT'S BEST TO AVOID ANY FORM OF MENTAL ACTIVITY.

STAFF MEETING!

Panel 4: LET ME SHOW YOU WHERE THE INFORMATION IS IN YOUR BINDER.

Panel 5: FIRST, I'LL NEED A GOOD LOAD OF SALIVA ON MY PAGE-TURNING HAND.

SLURP SLURP

Panel 6: MAYBE YOU CAN SHOW ME IN YOUR BINDER.

CAN'T... SOMEHOW MY PAGES GOT ALL STUCK TOGETHER.

Panel 7: IT'S AMAZING THAT PEOPLE BELIEVE IN ASTROLOGY... AS IF THE STARS COULD AFFECT YOUR PERSONALITY.

Panel 8: WELL, SEASONAL DIFFERENCES IN DIET, SUNLIGHT AND NATURAL RHYTHMS COULD AFFECT EXPECTANT MOTHERS, WHICH COULD HAVE PREDICTABLE RESULTS ON FETAL BRAIN DEVELOPMENT.

Panel 9: MAYBE THE ANCIENTS SIMPLY USED THE STARS TO MEASURE THE TIMING OF THESE PATTERNS.

IF THEY WERE SO SMART, WHY DIDN'T THEY INVENT WATCHES?

I'VE FAILED THE DRIVING TEST NINE TIMES. CAN YOU HELP?

DOGBERT'S DRIVING SCHOOL

I SPECIALIZE IN THE PROBLEM CASES. JUST SIGN THE APPLICATION FORM.

WAIT... I'VE SEEN ONE OF THESE BEFORE. YES, THERE'S SOMETHING SPECIAL ABOUT THE POINTY END... BUT WHAT?

UH OH

SIGN ME UP, LITTLE DOGGIE-DUDE.

DOGBERT'S DRIVING SCHOOL

WE'LL BEGIN WITH A FILM ABOUT GRUESOME HIGHWAY ACCIDENTS. IT IS INTENDED TO SHOCK YOU INTO DRIVING SAFELY.

REALLY? PEOPLE GET SHOCKED BY THIS?

I'LL BE FOLLOWING YOUR CAR IN A HELICOPTER.

WITH YOUR RIGHT HAND, INSERT A CD INTO THE STEREO... GOOD.

STUDENT DRIVER

NOW SIGNAL LEFT! ANSWER THE CAR PHONE! DEFROST THE REAR WINDOW! HONK IF YOU LOVE FISHING!

FORTUNATELY, WE'RE ONLY IN THE DRIVING SIMULATOR.

DO YOU BOYS WANT TO TAKE IT FOR A TEST DRIVE?

SALE

SOMETIMES I WORRY THAT I'LL NEVER BE CREATIVE AGAIN. MAYBE MY BEST IDEAS ARE BEHIND ME.

OH, I WOULDN'T WORRY. NOTHING YOU'VE DONE UP TO NOW HAS BEEN ANY GREAT SHAKES EITHER.

OOH, SO MAYBE MY BEST WORK IS STILL AHEAD OF ME.

WELL, YOU HAVE TO CONSIDER THE TRACK RECORD HERE.

MY PROBLEM IS THAT OTHER PEOPLE KEEP TRYING TO DRAG ME DOWN, BOB.

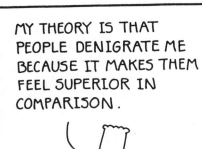

MY THEORY IS THAT PEOPLE DENIGRATE ME BECAUSE IT MAKES THEM FEEL SUPERIOR IN COMPARISON.

SOUNDS LIKE A STUPID THEORY TO ME.

WHY ARE YOU SO GLUM?

IT'S LONELY WHEN DOGBERT IS AWAY.

LONELY? HA! LET ME ENTERTAIN YOU WITH A LITTLE DANCE NUMBER. THEN WE'LL BOND AND I'LL REPLACE DOGBERT AS YOUR BEST FRIEND!

NOW I'M LONELY AND I HAVE A DANCING RAT.

KUMBAYA

WHAT HAPPENED TO YOU?

I ASKED FLOYD A QUESTION.

FLOYD HATES HIS JOB, SO HE TAKES IT OUT ON CO-WORKERS. HE ALMOST CHEWED MY CLOTHES OFF.

11-9

HOW'D YOU STOP HIM?

HE WENT INTO SYNTHETIC SHOCK; IT'S NOT HEALTHY TO EAT TOO MUCH OF THIS STUFF.

WHAT?! YOU THINK I'LL HELP YOU JUST BECAUSE I'M YOUR CO-WORKER?? HA! I HATE CO-WORKERS!

ALL I NEED IS...

I HATE THIS JOB! I HATE EVERYTHING! THE ONLY THING I LIKE IS BEING MEAN TO CO-WORKERS WHO NEED THE VITAL INFORMATION THAT I CONTROL!

11-10

IF YOU THINK YOU HATE HIM, YOU SHOULD TRY BEING HIS SECRETARY.

EVERYBODY PICK A STRAW. THE LOSER HAS TO KILL OUR ABUSIVE CO-WORK-ER, FLOYD.

11-11

DILBERT LOSES. HE PICKED THE BLUE STRAW.

I THOUGHT THE SHORT STRAW LOSES.

YOU'RE ALREADY A MURDERER; DON'T BE A CHEAT-ER TOO.

THE GUYS IN THE OFFICE DECIDED THAT SOMEBODY MUST KILL FLOYD THE BUDGET MANAGER BECAUSE HE'S SO MEAN TO US.

THEY WANT ME TO KILL HIM. BUT I CAN'T DO IT. I'M A LOVER, NOT A KILLER.

11-12

TECHNICALLY, YOU'RE NEITHER.

IS THAT MY FAULT?

I'VE GOT TO TELL YOU, FLOYD, THAT YOUR CO-WORKERS ARE SO FED UP WITH YOUR ATTITUDE THAT THEY ASKED ME TO ... UH ... KILL YOU.

WHAT??!

HEH-HEH ... OF COURSE THERE'S NO WAY I'D ACTUALLY ...

ERK! MMPH ...

11-13

I'M REALLY GOING TO HAVE TO DRESS THIS UP ON MY QUARTERLY ACCOMPLISHMENT REPORT.

WE HEARD YOU KILLED FLOYD, OUR UNBEARABLE CO-WORKER, YESTERDAY.

NO. I WAS THERE, BUT HE CHOKED ON HIS OWN BILE.

11-14

WHAT DID YOU DO — PERFORM FIRST AID? CALL AN AMBULANCE?

I DON'T KNOW FIRST AID.

UH ... CAN I USE YOUR PHONE?

DILBERT

By Scott Adams

WAITER, THERE'S A HAIR IN MY SOUP.

IT LOOKS LIKE ONE OF YOURS. I'M SURE IT WASN'T THERE WHEN I SERVED IT.

IT IS **NOT** ONE OF MINE!

SIR! YOU INSULT MY INTEGRITY!

I SHALL SEND THE HAIR TO OUR LAB FOR ANALYSIS.

FAIR ENOUGH.

THEY'LL NEED A CLUMP OF YOUR HAIR FOR COMPARISON.

OUCH!

YOU HAVE TO BE TOUGH WITH THESE WAITERS OR ELSE THEY'LL WALK ALL OVER YOU.

DOES IT SEEM ODD TO YOU THAT THE RESTAURANT HAS ITS OWN LAB?

THEY MUST HAVE A LOT OF PROBLEMS WITH HAIRY FOOD.

THE LAB SAYS THEY NEED A FEW MORE CLUMPS OF YOUR HAIR...

11-15

S. Adams

THE TINY NATION OF ELBONIA HAS ERUPTED IN CIVIL WAR.

WHAT CAUSED YOU TO TURN YOUR WEAPONS ON YOUR OWN PEOPLE?

WEAPONS? WE CAN USE WEAPONS?

WELL, NO WONDER IT WAS TAKING SO LONG.

THE PRESIDENT OF ELBONIA ASKED ME TO NEGOTIATE AN END TO THEIR CIVIL WAR.

WHY YOU?

NO DOUBT HE WAS IMPRESSED BY MY DIPLOMACY WHEN I WAS AN ECONOMIC ADVISOR... I JUST WISH I DIDN'T HAVE TO FLY ON ELBONIA AIRLINES.

ELBONIA

...AT HIS WEIGHT, WE CALCULATE THAT ELBONIA AIRLINES WILL FLING HIM RIGHT ON THE REBEL LEADER.

DILBERT TAKES ELBONIA AIRLINES. HE'S BEEN ASKED TO NEGOTIATE AN END TO THE ELBONIAN CIVIL WAR.

I CAN SUCCEED IF I FIND SOME WAY TO IMPRESS THE REBEL LEADER THEY CALL "THE FOX."

THE FOX IS DEAD!!

DILBERT

By Scott Adams

DOGBERT'S SCHOOL FOR JERKS

HEY!

WE'LL BEGIN BY SORTING YOU INTO THE THREE MAJOR JERK CATEGORIES FOR SPECIALIZED INSTRUCTION.

LOOK AT THIS PICTURE OF SUPERMODEL CINDY CRAWFORD.

WHOA! HUBBA! SNORT!

ANYBODY WHO SAID "HUBBA" STAND OVER THERE. YOU ARE WHAT IS CALLED "JERKS AROUND WOMEN."

NOW, SOMEBODY CATCH THIS BALL, PLEASE.

FOUL! YOU FOULED!

ANYBODY WHO YELLED "FOUL" IS A "SPORTS JERK." STAND OVER THERE.

IT WAS A FOUL.

S. Adams

SO, WHOEVER IS LEFT MUST BE...

11-22

HURRY UP. I'M LATE FOR COURT.

YOU'RE A LAWYER TOO?

I WAS GOING TO SAY "HUBBA."

© 1992 United Feature Syndicate, Inc.

WE LEFT-HANDED ELBONIANS HAVE BEEN PERSECUTED FOR CENTURIES. WE MUST CRUSH THE RIGHTIES!

DON'T YOU SEE THAT IT'S ONLY AN ARBITRARY DISTINCTION? ISN'T IT OBVIOUS THAT PEOPLE ARE THE SAME NO MATTER WHAT HAND THEY FAVOR?

11-23

NO, THAT ISN'T OBVIOUS TO US AT ALL.

GEEZ, YOU LEFTIES ARE THICK. I'M GLAD I'M NORMAL.

ELBONIANS HEAR ME! YOU MUST END YOUR FUTILE CIVIL WAR.

YOU'VE BEEN LOVING YOUR ANIMALS AND FIGHTING EACH OTHER. A CIVILIZED COUNTRY SHOULD SLAUGHTER THE ANIMALS AND SIMPLY DISCRIMINATE ECONOMICALLY AGAINST EACH OTHER!

HOW DID MY SPEECH GO OVER?

I'M SOLD, BUT I THINK THE SECRETARY OF STATE WAS A BIT PUT OFF.

11-24

I ALWAYS THOUGHT YOU BEAVERS WERE BUSY ALL THE TIME.

THAT'S A COMMON STEREOTYPE. I'M ACTUALLY QUITE LAZY.

HOW DO YOU BUILD YOUR BEAVER HOME?

I RENT.

11-25

WHEN YOU'RE A LAZY BEAVER, YOU TRY TO FIND SHORTCUTS AND TRICKS TO GET YOUR WORK DONE.

I GOT THIS DAYTIME PLANNER TO ORGANIZE MY DAY MORE EFFICIENTLY.

BUT ALL IT DOES IS SIT THERE.

LOOKS LIKE YOU GOT A BAD ONE.

11-26

JUST TAKE ONE, RATBERT.

11-27

AAARGH!! I'M CHANGING! I'M CHANGING!

IT WASN'T FUNNY THE FIRST HUNDRED TIMES I GAVE YOU A TIC-TAC EITHER.

LET'S TRY IT AGAIN!

THE ROOF IS LEAKING THERE. CAN YOU FIX IT TOMORROW?

WELL, LIKE ALL MEMBERS OF MY PROFESSION, I'M UNRELIABLE. HOWEVER, I COULD GIVE YOU A QUOTE AND THEN NEVER SHOW UP OR RETURN YOUR CALLS.

YOU'RE HIRED. NOBODY ELSE WOULD EVEN SHOW UP FOR THE QUOTE.

I DEPEND ON REPEAT CUSTOMERS.

11-28

DILBERT

By Scott Adams

I DISCOVERED A NEW TOOL FOR MEETING WOMEN.

A METAL DETECTOR?

EXACTLY. I'LL BE NONCHALANTLY USING IT IN THE PARK...

AND YOU'LL FIND BURIED WOMEN WHO HAVE METAL PLATES IN THEIR HEADS?

DON'T BE RIDICULOUS. THE ODDS OF FINDING A LIVE ONE ARE ABOUT A JILLION TO ONE.

NO, I PLAN TO APPEAL TO WOMEN'S NATURAL SCIENTIFIC CURIOSITY.

THEY'LL STRIKE UP CONVERSATIONS ABOUT HOW THE METAL DETECTOR WORKS ... AND WHERE THEY CAN BUY ONE.

11-29

OOH, I'D BETTER BRING A NOTE PAD TO WRITE DOWN ALL THE PHONE NUMBERS.

ON ONE PAW, I WANT TO HELP HIM. ON THE OTHER PAW, MAYBE IT'S BETTER IF HE DOESN'T EVER REPRODUCE.

IN A SURPRISE DECISION, THE UNITED NATIONS VOTED TO MAKE DOGBERT— THE SPACE ALIEN — THE SUPREME RULER OF EARTH.

MORE ON THAT LATER. BUT FIRST, SCIENCE OFFERS NEW HOPE FOR PEOPLE WITH FRECKLES...

12-3

DOGBERT HOLDS HIS FIRST PRESS CONFERENCE

HU-HA-HA! HU-HA-HA!

NOT A GOOD SIGN.

NOW THAT YOU'RE THE SUPREME RULER OF EARTH, WILL YOU BECOME MORALLY CORRUPT?

YES, THAT'S MY PLAN. IT'S REALLY THE ONLY WAY TO ENJOY A JOB LIKE THIS.

12-4

AND OF COURSE I'LL BE RAISING TAXES JUST TO SEE THE EXPRESSIONS ON YOUR FACES.

STOP! I AM THE "AMAZING RONNY,". FAMOUS SKEPTIC AND DEBUNKER.

12-5

I WILL PROVE TO THE MEDIA THAT YOU'RE NOT A POWERFUL SPACE ALIEN AT ALL.

SEE HOW EASILY THE MEDIA WERE DUPED?

THERE'S STILL TIME TO INTER- VIEW THE COW WHO DOES ALGE- BRA.

RRRR

DILBERT

By Scott Adams

DOGBERT'S HOME SAFETY TIPS

IT COULD SAVE YOUR LIFE!

TIP #1: CHILDREN CAN SWALLOW ANYTHING SMALLER THAN A SOFA. ATTACH BOARDS TO VULNERABLE APPLIANCES.

HA HA! NICE TRY, BILLY!

MMPH!

TIP #2: YOUR HOUSEHOLD MAY HAVE A MEMBER WHO CAN LEGALLY VOTE BUT PROBABLY SHOULDN'T.

TRY TRICKING THEM INTO MISSING THE ELECTION.

WE'RE A COMMUNIST REGIME NOW. YOU DON'T HAVE TO VOTE.

SHOOT!

TIP #3: YOUR TELEVISION IS TRYING TO STEAL YOUR LIFE'S SAVINGS.

I PERSONALLY PRAY OVER EVERY CHECK YOU SEND.

YOUR ONLY HOPE IS TO PUSH YOUR TELEVISION OUT A HIGH WINDOW.

IF EVERYBODY DOES IT, WE JUST MIGHT GET LUCKY.

S. Adams

12-6

WHAT'S THE STORY WITH THE COSTUME, WALLY?

THE BOSS PUT ME ON A SPECIAL TASK FORCE TO SEE IF HUMOR INCREASES CREATIVITY. I HAVE TO DRESS LIKE THIS FOR A MONTH.

ARE YOU FEELING MORE CREATIVE?

YEAH. I'VE ALREADY THOUGHT OF SIX HUNDRED WAYS TO KILL HIM.

AS PART OF MY PROGRAM TO USE MORE HUMOR AT WORK, I'M ASKING EACH OF YOU TO WEAR A "KICK ME" SIGN.

I'LL CHECK LATER TO SEE IF YOU'RE MORE RELAXED AND CREATIVE.

LATER...

YOU SEEM TO BE TAKING UNFAIR ADVANTAGE OF THE SITUATION, ALICE.

OUR VIDEO GAME DIVISION HAS REACHED A SALES PLATEAU.

KIDS ARE SPENDING MORE TIME OUTSIDE THESE DAYS. THERE'S ONLY ONE THING WE CAN DO.

DIVERSIFY?

POLLUTE!

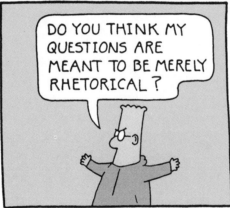

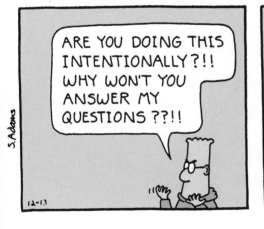